The Sky Between Us

And the Voices That Bind Us

Three Sisters ||| Three Voices

KI Sutphin, CS Norwood, and SL Malvoso

PUBLISHERS CATALOGING-IN-PUBLICATION DATA

The Sky Between Us: And the Voices That Bind Us

Three sisters, three voices

This book is a collaborative work of original poetry, prose, and shared memory.

Sections authored by KI Sutphin, CS Norwood, and SL Malvoso are original and human-created.

LITERARY COLLECTIONS / Subjects & Themes / General / Animals and Nature
POETRY / Subjects & Themes / General / Haiku

Paperback

167 pages / 7 x 10 x 0.44 inches / 104 illustrations

First edition: April 2026

Library of Congress Control Number: 2026907154

ISBN: 979-8-9924305-8-5

Photos and Images by Pixabay are cited. Select editorial and layout support, including image generation and formatting guidance, was provided by AI assistant "Jack" (Microsoft Copilot) or individual artist or photographer.

All AI-generated content is clearly marked and used with permission.

Cover Design by CS Norwood and KI Sutphin

Printed in the United States of America

For permissions, inquiries, or archival requests, contact:

carolan@station-wil.com

Scan the QR Code to visit us on the web at Station WIL. This book is published by

AWI adventure writers ink
Bay Minette | Twin Falls

DEDICATION

To readers, writers, and storytellers everywhere.

INTRODUCTION

The same sky above us, but many years and miles between us, we three sisters have come together to share our voices—created over decades, shaped by different journeys, different world views, different joys and sorrows.

This collection brings together adventure stories, imagined worlds, and poems that reflect without lingering in shadow. Each piece stands on its own, yet together they trace the arc of how we've lived, dreamed, and made meaning across the years. Some of these pages look outward—toward journeys, choices, and the unpredictable terrain of real life. Others look inward or sideways, into realms where animals speak, storms have opinions, and the impossible feels just within reach. What binds them is not a single theme, but the simple truth that creativity has always been our meeting place.

We offer this collection as a constellation: separate lights, distant at times, yet unmistakably part of the same sky.

CONTENTS

THE SKY BETWEEN US:
And the Voices That Bind Us

Three Sisters ||| Three Voices

Face to the Rain

by KI Sutphin

Face to the Rain reflects my progression from childhood pain to playfulness and a strengthening trust in God. In early years, soul-drenching hikes in the rain, talking to critters along the way, allowed me to escape the tempest inside.

In middle years I realized the path forward was drawn for me by God's helping hand. Through faith in His love and with the counsel of critters, I took one step and then another.

Today, a rainy walk in the woods is a refreshing time for reflection and thankfulness. The critters along my path continue to advise me to believe in myself, trust in God's plan and enjoy each footstep along the way — without regrets, only lessons learned.

Face to the Rain

The Storm Within

Face to the Rain

Not a gentle touch
        more persistent
                demanding
                        determined to reach its end.

Out of grayness
        a feeling of purpose
                washing over me
                        a quenching downpour.

My thoughts are flooded
        the answers swirling
                beyond my reach
                        my soul is wanting ... another storm.

The Place Inside

There is a shelter deep inside my head, a solitary place
Far from daily grind, a quiet place
Exposed without my mask, a safe place

To consider the existence that I lead
To stimulate my senses
To play the games I missed in childhood

And wonder why I am.

Rain Dance

The trees flutter in anticipation of the storm's arrival
Racing to the meadow, arms
outstretched
Dancing to the rumbled drumbeat

Autumn colors floating past my fingertips
Entranced by their gentle beauty
Unaware of danger

Penny for Your Thoughts

A house full of haunts
A pool full of tears
A heart packed with sorrow
A life lived in fear

Collections of feelings
The fortune is vast
High price for this treasure
The sins of our past

In the Distance

Can't you see it
in the distance, through the fog?

The mist is clearing
My journey ending

My body weary
I am exhausted

Can my past reflect my future
in the distance, through the fog.

Mist

As dawn breaks in my rearview mirror, I speed on my way

A mist hovers lazily over the roadside pond
No notice to my passing.

Storm

A line of dark clouds backlit by lightning
There is tension in the still air ...
Waiting

A bolt of lightning pauses in the clouds
The power is awesome in the still air ...
Approaching

The wind is quicker now, the storm is near
Ozone fills my lungs in the darkness ...
Breathing

The storm is overhead and in my soul
My feeble pleas for mercy drown in the echoes ...
Raging

Too quickly come and gone, there is a letdown
The sister storm moves on and I am alone again ...
Waiting

My Wet Foot

When I walk through a storm
I risk the lightning, risk the pain.
Yet I am bound as is the lemming
To take that step that leads me home.

In the Daylight

In the daylight there is
An unkind darkness in my mind

Nothing I do can penetrate
The heavy shroud upon me

Others do not see the fear inside
Distracted by the radiance of their lives

Nothing I do can lift
This heavy shroud upon me

Inner Fight

There is a battle for my life
Fought inside my head
The defender speaks of kindness
The aggressor musters pain

There is a battle for my life
Fought inside my head
Anger, rage and bloodshed
Upon the cerebral plain

Soldiers armed and able
Committed to their cause
As darkness falls, the soldiers too
The battle won, the winner yet unknown.

Fading

The light fades from my day
My love weakens like blood rushing from my head
Draining from my heart and soul
The wounds too deep
The trust broken
My passion a fantasy
Forever alone
In darkness
Safe

A Prayer

Sprawled by my bedside, I am lost and alone.
Sprawled in the darkness, my tears wet the carpet.
Sprawled without answers, I beg once again.
Please forgive me all my sins, there are so many.
Watch over those I love, send angels to protect them.
Remember those I've wronged, help them on their way.
Help me stand and face another day.

The Pit

I fell into the pitty pit
That deep foreboding hole
Trapped and cold and desparit
My dark, imploding soul

Enough

I'm not sure why Jesus loves me, although I am assured.
Is that a childish ploy to keep me in the faith?
Believe enough, you are addicted to the taste.

Yes Jesus loves me, although I've faltered many times.
Is that the way I show my love, to promise and recant?
If only Jesus loved me, no one else, is that enough for me?

The Butterfly

Delicate orange and black, fleeting in my path
Speeding along, it's tiny impact unfelt by me
No notice by anyone, no trace of loss
Still, an unquiet sense ... the universe shuddered.

The Red Bird

High atop the dead wood tree,
a red bird perched to sing for me
Its gentle aria, perfection by design
Sang for tiny flowers and rutting deer and me.

The Puddle

Splash, splash, splash,
Let's stomp in the puddle and skip in the rain.

Splash, splash, splash,
Let's dance in the raindrops and sing with the storm.

Splash, splash, splash,
Let's stomp out our footprints til they dry in the sun.

Splash, splash, splash,
Let's remember this moment and smile when we're done.

Move On

A little turtle spoke to me
It asked me if I heard
How little perch got hooked on flies
Then left without a word.

A little turtle spoke to me
To tell me of its crime
It ate the last of minnows
Its tummy felt sublime.

A little turtle spoke to me
It wanted me to know
Its life was filled with purpose
Get up, it said, and go.

Patience

The moment was perfect as I crouched beside the still water.
Instantly, a tiny frog face emerged to break the surface tension.
Motionless as we could be, we waited for a low-flying bug
But then a snake came racing by ~
and me, the frog were history.

Tree Hugger

The hike stretched hilly and long
The tree stood impatiently waiting
As if a lifetime passed between us.

It leaned into my path
And I bowed without speaking
As if a lifetime weighed on weary shoulders.

The wind hesitated to watch
The tree stood waiting
As if embrace could heal our mossy scars.

I said goodbye dear friend
We knew forever without saying
A lifetime passed between us.

Worry Stone

That simple, smooth, symmetric, palm full of nothing
Why this rock chosen from the riverbed's stony galaxy?
An ordinary stone and yet with purpose given
No other one would do.

The River

Carving a course with the force of its flow
Dancing, gurgling, spilling from moment to moment.

Rushing without notice
Nourishing, cooling, reflecting its passage.

Advice

The rain ran down my pant leg
It jumped into a pool
It swam around in circles
And yelled I was a fool.

I asked it why the comment
It backstroked with such skill
I thought it was Olympian
It said I had no will.

I stepped into the puddle
The raindrop raced for shore
I vowed I was the stronger
It said I was a bore.

We sat upon an ancient rock
It glistened in the sun
My life was full of hopes and dreams
But actions, I had none.

The shadows slowly lengthened
They vanished with the sun
I hurried home to start anew
A course that I could run.

I look for dark clouds in the West
To bring that small, wet voice
Whose wisdom spoke in fleeting breaths,
Be brave and make a choice.

Fate and Faith

A tiny snail sped out in front of me
Its course a concrete wasteland warming in the sun
It had no long range vision, its path to bake in route.

I stopped to wonder could this be my fate,
Was this the plan today?
To spare this tiny gastropod its certain, deadly destiny?

I stooped to touch its tiny shell and lift it to the grass.
Life's made of tiny moments sewn with silver threads.
Its fate was in the balance, as mine was in God's hands.

Growing

Positive energy rushes through my body like a springtime flood
New channels form as gritty doubt,
despair and baggage give way
A tiny crocus, a new thought, pushes into consciousness

On Bended Knee

Light

Through the darkness I see a light
Could it be a distant sun?
Too far to feel its warmth
A pinhole of hope in my curtain of madness

Reaching Within

Are you there little one?
Can I reach you?

Are there memories
To be shared?

Will you teach me
Of the pain that I've been spared.

Will you speak of what you've suffered?
Please release me from my suffering if you dare.

Seeing

My mind's eye opens
It stares into my soul
My breathing slows

There is much to know
I do not apologize
I cannot cry

Without intention
There is no meter
The depth of years unknown

Ownership

Like the early morning dawn
An awakening, a realization
Having is not loving

Blame

I am embarrassed to face my failures
Wanting to find fault outside myself
Old enough to know better
Ignoring the soft tick, tick, tick
Trying to correct the past
Instead repeating it
Choices are just that.

Renewal

The air fills with the moisture of renewal
The earth laps up each droplet with a joy
that blossoms on its skin.
The breeze picks up the damp melody
Washing it over my weathered soul.

Wake Up Call

I asked and when He answered,
I did not understand the message.
I fell and did not feel His hand when He picked me up to take another step.
I lived a life of regrets and blame without knowing it could be different.
And now at last I see, I know, I feel, I hope it's not too late to change.

On My Knees

On my knees, I beg forgiveness
On my knees I ask for help
Your mercy is the hand
That pulls me up and makes me stand.

Hold My Hand

Go with me into the evening,
holding my hand,
sharing the touch,
feeling the promise
of what lays beyond.

Go with me into tomorrow
keeping me safe,
sharing each moment,
dreaming beside me
until it must end.

Forsaken

Do not forsake me oh my savior,
An old tune pleads with you.
Do not forsake me my beloved
I am weak and need renewed.

Do not mistake me for an answer,
My thoughts are muddied and disturbed.
Do not mistake me for your purpose,
I am tired and so confused.

Do not rebuke me for my failings,
I never promised to be perfect.
Do not berate me my redeemer
My sins are many and continued.

Do not forget me on my passing.
I cannot leave unless you know
That in our meeting I am whole.
On bended knee, I bow to you.

Meditating, reaching, first gently, then deeply
Fearing, yet wanting answers, searching for meaning
Knowing secrets buried may never be told

With a rhythm washing like ocean tides into my consciousness,
A whale's eye appears—ancient, with wisdom seasoned by
life's ebb and flow
Challenging, almost dismissive, it tells me go and do.

Soul Wash

Attentively I listen; the sermon winds on
There they are, two angels perched on the pew in front of me
No one noticing but me
Sudsy buckets in hand, distracting me from communion

What are you doing? Why are you here?
Smiling, without speaking, brushes slop in holy water
Reaching deep, scrubbing hard
It's springtime; you are overdue.

Quietly reaching the far corners of my soul
Cob webs and sorrow, sins and regrets
I am soaked, I am baptized
With God's love I am blessed; through His grace I am saved.

The Calling

She died suddenly, violently—her sweet voice, her soul's melody, stolen from me in the night. Although my mother's assailant was known to all, he was never caught—forever in the wind and free to kill again. As protection, I locked myself into a virtual prison created by fear. I didn't travel. I skipped family gatherings—no more nighttime concerts, no more dinner parties with my friends, and, worst of all, no more singing.

Today, at breakfast, a tiny kernel of corn stuck in my throat. I couldn't breathe. Bent over, wheezing and hacking, I finally cleared my airway. Besides freeing that gritty morsel, I coughed up something bigger, a grain of common sense. I laughed, declaring to myself, "I'm such a birdbrain."

Worries of what might happen were eating away at me like a cancer. My mother died suddenly, but I was dying slowly—a death of my own making. Drained of joy, missing opportunities, losing friends, a fear of dying had developed into a fear of living. I needed to fix that.

How to begin? I was ready to sing, but who would listen? Fluffing my feathers for warmth, I stared at the icy glaze blanketing a field of broken cornstalks. At the first snowfall, my father and sisters flew south to the milder climate of the Sierra Madre Mountains of northern Mexico. That left me alone except for a few winter-weather friends.

With any luck, Mariel and Rudy were huddled in the brushy thickets surrounding the frosty cornfield. I scanned the treetops searching for Rudy's bright red coat. After several unanswered tweets, I heard Mariel's chirpy reply.

"What's up, Lucie?"

I quickly returned the chirp. "Can we chat? I'm sorry I've been so withdrawn. Are we still friends?"

Her immediate answer sounded cheery. "Of course we are. You're my friend, always. Meet me at the watering hole. I have lots to tell you."

Nodding my head to no one but myself, I agreed. "Great. I'm on my way."

Except during Texas gully-washer rainstorms, the watering hole remained a small puddle replenished by a trickle from an underground spring. The surrounding mix of muhly grass, dull-green junipers, and spiny desert agaritas stripped of their berries offered shade and protection for those who came to drink.

Moments later, I settled at the water's edge. With each swallow, my scruffy reflection waved outward, slowly disappearing into the shallows, a watery image of myself. After several refreshing gulps, I hopped beneath the slender fronds of nearby muhly grass. It was a private, windless spot for us to talk.

Mariel arrived quickly, but to my surprise, she was alone. "Where's Rudy? You two are always together."

Mariel leapt close to me, her approach as bouncy as her speech. "Oh, he's keeping watch from the juniper. He'll give us a whistle if he spies danger."

As I began an explanation for my absence, Mariel interrupted.

She had neighborhood news to share. I sighed as she began. "You'll never guess. Chickee's cousin flew in from the Sangre de Cristo Mountains. It's funny. He spends more time hoarding juniper seeds than visiting with Chickee.

Rudy and I watched him hide hundreds of seeds in one of the knotholes on that old cottonwood on the west side of the arroyo. And then, while he was busy searching for more seeds, the squirrels rushed in to pilfer his stash."

I chuckled and started to tweet, but Mariel had more to share. "Then late yesterday, we watched a large rattlesnake fall from the clutches of a large red hawk. Splat! The snake hit the rock pile in the center of the field. By morning, its bloodied carcass had been ripped apart, probably by the old possum that burrows under the rocks."

"On seeing that assassin, Rudy whistled out a warning. This was the first time we've seen that copper-tailed demon. I think that it has claimed our neighborhood as its hunting ground."

At this revelation, my whole body quivered. Mariel stopped talking and stared at me. She must have realized that the same kind of predator had taken my mother. Again, I was face-to-face with the ordeal and pain of her loss. I breathed slowly, then muttered to myself, "Let it go."

Mariel draped her soft-brown wing over my shoulder. I leaned toward her and whispered, "I'm okay."

Although I didn't feel thankful for Mariel's update, I spoke the words. "Thanks for sharing. I've been away for too long. When my mother disappeared, it felt like I was dead too. One feather, that's all I had of her—a keepsake of my anger and fear. Finally, I understood that I couldn't change what had happened. But the pain of yesterday shouldn't control me today. I needed to find a place for her in my heart and let go of the grief."

A still moment passed between us before I withdrew and spread my wings. "Tada, here I am. I want to sing again."

Mariel bounced toward me. "Great, I'm glad you're here. We have work to do."

She began hopping in circles, scattering desert dust as she spun. Laughing, I joined her dance. "Mariel, exactly what work are you talking about?"

She stopped abruptly and turned to me, beak-to-beak. "You want to sing; you need to sing. Your bright staccato cuts through the daylight chatter like the blade of the farmer's plow and pierces the night like a bolt of lightning. Your powerful voice is your gift—so use it, develop it, and you will sing again."

My eyelids closed as tears cleared the dust. "Really, a farmer's plow? But you're right, Mariel. I have squandered the best part of me. Help me fix that."

She hopped close again, beak-to-beak—hers a vivid orange, demanding my attention. "We're going on tour."

I couldn't believe her. "What are you talking about? I am not prepared to sing to myself, much less to a flock of unappreciative old crows." I turned my back on her.

"Stop that. Look at me. I'm not asking you to perform. I'm asking you to listen."

I spun around. "Listen to what? I don't understand."

"We need help from Chickee's cousin. When he's not hoarding seeds, he talks of a city beyond the mountains, a city with incredible twilight tweets, trills, and warbles. We're going to ask him to guide us there. You must leave your field and forest songs and search out these amazing new sounds. Gather them as Coronell gathers the juniper seeds. Practice them; perform them. It is your destiny."

This was too much for me. Angrily, I asked, "What do you know about my destiny?"

"Remember, your mother and I were best friends. She often tweeted about your special voice, with a range crisper, broader, and faster than most mockingbirds. In her view, you were wasted on this farmland. When she was stolen from us, I promised myself that I would help you find your voice. It isn't here. It's out there, beyond the mountains. Let's talk to Coronell."

I watched Mariel flit off to the juniper grove to find Chickee's cousin. I guessed he was either eating seeds or stuffing them into a knothole. After building a flimsy nest from a few strands of dry grass, I fluffed my feathers, closed my eyes, and settled on my cold feet to wait for their return.

Mariel's cheer-cheer-cheer call startled me awake and announced their arrival. She and Coronell joined me in my crude nest within the frozen safety of the muhly grass. The fading winter sun did little to warm us as a cold wind whirled across the landscape. Mariel fluffed her feathers and then turned to our guest.

"Coronell, thank you for agreeing to lead us westward to the mountains beyond the high desert. As I told you, Lucie and I are anxious to listen to the mysterious songs of your homeland."

Coronell dropped several juniper seeds on the ground before advising us. "We have a long and treacherous journey ahead. Leaving now would risk a snowstorm that would weigh us down and hide the food necessary to fuel our bodies. We must wait for the mild Spring winds. Until then, strengthen your wings and your resolve. You must commit to the journey. Once we begin our flight to the mountains, I will not turn back."

Without speaking, Mariel turned to me and waited. Questions churned in my head. Was my hesitation common sense or lingering fear? Was I strong enough, brave enough to dare? Would this be one more missed opportunity? My bird brain didn't have answers, but my heart did. I tweeted my decision. "Let's do it."

I devoted weeks flying back and forth over the barren cornfield, strengthening my flight muscles, practicing my trills, and occasionally stealing juniper seeds from Coronell's stash. The days were getting longer, and my friends and I were getting noisier. Also, I noticed a change in the air; it was lighter, warmer. I hurried to find Coronell. In between snacking, he pointed to the reddish buds on the branches of the cottonwood—an early sign of Spring. "Find Mariel. It's time to fly."

Mariel and Rudy were resting high in the juniper overlooking the watering hole. She didn't seem excited when I shared that Coronell was ready to head home. In a sullen chirp, she asked, "Could we talk alone? Let's get a drink."

I waited for her to sip from the shallow pool before springing into our hideaway. She quickly explained her solemn tone. "I'm sorry, Lucie, but I can't go with you. I'm worried for Rudy. His eyes are swollen and crusty, making it hard for him to find food. I can't leave him alone. I hope you understand. You and Coronell will have to travel without me."

I wanted to scream. It was her idea for us to make this journey. She was the one who convinced me that my destiny lay beyond the mountains. And now, I had to do it without her. The we was now me. I sat quietly, digesting the situation. "I'm sorry, too, but I understand. You are committed to Rudy, as I suppose I am committed to this journey."

When I turned from our grassy retreat, I caught a soft tweet, "Sing, dear Lucie, sing."

Coronell and I lifted off before the sun rose above the horizon. My small wings can go fast but not far. By noon, I was exhausted and thirsty. We found a small pond where we took several refreshing gulps. I nabbed a passing beetle when Coronell chided me. "We must keep going. We need to get to that distant juniper stand before dark. Then we can eat."

Hazy clouds blocked the western sun as we reached our waypoint. I was thankful for the food and comfort it provided. We nestled our weary bodies among the fan-like juniper leaves and waited for daybreak.

From sun-up to sundown, our daylight routine was the same: gliding, resting when we needed, eating what we could, wings flapping, muscles aching. After a few tedious days, we cleared the high desert. I was grateful when Coronell agreed to rest at the base of the mountains before finishing the journey over the dark peaks of evergreen forests.

The next morning, soft gray rain clouds drifted in the distance as we crested the mountains. We rested on a white fir tree to take in the landscape beneath us—a meandering river, rugged mesas, thick woodlands. Coronell happily chirped, "My journey has ended. My home is here, in the mountains. Yours is below, set in the foothills among the budding aspens. Be patient, and the city will sing to you.

As Coronell disappeared into the dense forest, I recognized that I was alone and far from home. The feeling proved both frightening and thrilling. I dived from the treetop to search out a new home, and, hopefully, a new life filled with song.

By midday, I found a nesting site near a steep-sided arroyo lined with dense shrubs. I discovered a few small dark olives hiding deep in thick branches, a perfect place for food and safety. After a day of collecting sticks and grass, I burrowed into my twiggy nest and closed my eyes. Now, as Mariel suggested, I had to wait and listen for the nighttime melodies.

It took several days to establish my territory, warning off a white-winged dove and a pair of robins. Then, each night, I listened, but I only heard the sounds of the forest. And every morning, I rested on a tall juniper that offered plenty of breakfast berries. I scanned the city in the distance. Perhaps I was too far away to hear its music. Yes, I needed to move closer.

After a day of scouting neighborhood gardens sprinkled throughout the city, I rested on a rustic fencepost. My new life was beginning to feel like my old one. That's when I heard it—one piercing bird-like tone. It was coming from an open window behind an Apache plume dotted with tiny yellow butterflies. As I hid in the colorful shrubbery, a stream of staccato notes shook me from my perch. Unable to resist, I hopped to the windowsill and listened.

"Shoo, shoo, go away." Flapping her hands, a young woman raced toward me and slammed the window shut. Shocked and afraid, I flew back to the fencepost and then returned to my nest in the foothills. That night, I realized what I had to do. I would claim the garden as my own, build a nest near the window, and wait for it to open. There had to be more music.

The next day, I returned to the fencepost to begin gathering sticks and grass. Throughout the day, I snacked on bees and butterflies as I assembled my new home in the Apache plume. At nightfall, I slept, exhausted and uninterrupted.

A dry morning breeze shook the leaves around me. Awake and hungry, I snatched a butterfly before I landed on the fencepost. From there, I could oversee my territory, which now included the window. It didn't take long for it to open. I swooped to the sill.

At first, lots of babble, then finally, a repetition of the notes from yesterday. I was stunned by the intensity and rapid-fire vocal leaps. Suddenly, an older woman approached the window. She stomped her cane. I didn't flinch, and before she could say shoo, I repeated the high-pitched staccato.

She leaned toward me. "Aren't you a sweet thing?" With that, something fantastic happened.

I answered. "No one has ever called me sweet, more often, smart, determined, a great singer, but never sweet. How is it possible that we can communicate?"

"It is a magical blessing, a gift I've held since childhood. I can't explain it, perhaps a sense not yet defined by science. My name is Sofia. What's yours?"

"Lucie. I've traveled from beyond the mountains to listen to the music of your city."

She smiled. "I'm glad you came. Stay, please. I want my daughter to hear you sing." She turned away and yelled, "Sylvia, come to the kitchen. I want you to meet Lucie."

Standing behind her mother, Sylvia growled. "Is this bird another one of your chatty friends?"

Sofia pointed her cane toward me. "Go ahead, Lucie." Then to her daughter, "You listen."

My turn to smile. Her challenge to Sylvia reminded me of the same order from Mariel. I cleared my throat and repeated the attention-grabbing notes.

Sylvia fell back and stammered. "Ask her to sing that again." When I did, she joined me. For several minutes, I would follow Sylvia's vocalizations, playing back the sharp, staccato bursts that imitate familiar bird calls.

Needing to rest her voice box, Sylvia stopped and spoke to her mother. "I have a hair-brained idea, no, make that a bird-brained idea. We have a new stage director for our production of Mozart's The Magic Flute. He wants a novel presentation of this famous operatic comedy. What if your bird could join me in my role as Queen of the Night? We could echo the F6 notes together. That would be funny and amazing. I'm sure we could also cast Lucie in the opening scenes."

Sofia laughed, turned to me, and lifted a questioning eyebrow.

No need to think about it. I chirped my response. "It is my destiny."

Each morning, I sat on the windowsill and sang, sometimes Sylvia's aria, sometimes my own twist on her music. After several days, she announced the director's response to her idea. He loved that a real bird, with a range beyond that of any coloratura soprano, could be part of the performance. But before he could authorize it, the conductor needed to hear me sing.

I refused the birdcage Sylvia offered for our trip to the theater. Instead, I insisted that her mother join us as my translator and guardian. I would ride on her shoulder. Sylvia and Sofia stared at each other before nodding in unison.

"Okay," said Sofia, "but you must not panic. The theater can be swarming with performers and overwhelming with chaotic sounds as the orchestra rehearses."

I voiced my agreement.

After weeks of practice, it was time for the short trip to the theater. When we stepped from the car, the familiar feeling of fright and excitement clenched my hold on Sofia's shoulder. She winced and scolded, "Lighten up, little bird. You got this. You were born to sing."

The director greeted us at the door. "So, this is Lucia." When he reached out to touch me, we both pulled back. I heard him whisper to Sylvia, "The conductor is skeptical. As a challenge, he's assembled the full orchestra for the Queen of the Night aria.

"Quickly now, get into your costume, fluff your feathers, and be ready to sing in ten minutes."

I tugged at Sofia's ear, "My name is Lucie, not Lucia."

As she helped Sylvia dress in her glittering black gown, Sofia chided me. "Maybe it can be your stage name. Lucia has such an elegant ring to it." There was no time for Sylvia to fix her hair. Instead, she tied it into a topknot. "Here's your perch, Lucie-

Lucia. Let's go."

My body trembled when the orchestra struck its explosive opening chord. At that moment, Sylvia became the Queen of the Night, and I became Lucia, the queen's second voice, matching her pitch, duplicating her rapid-fire staccatos, climbing beyond the range of her human voice.

After our dramatic exit, Sylvia collapsed in her mother's arms, and I hopped on her mother's shoulder. We heard words of praise as the stage director and conductor approached us. "Bravissima! You captured the fury, the rage, the emotional intensity of the aria." The conductor clapped his hands. "We have much work to do before opening night."

The rehearsals were both grueling and invigorating. Although I required frequent beetle breaks, the conductor was lenient and instructive. I loved every musical morsel.

Sylvia had first-night jitters, but I was ready. As instructed, I flitted through the opening comedic scene shrieking like a banshee as I chased Tamino, the prince, across the stage. After that, I rested offstage on Sofia's shoulder, munching on raisins.

I waited for the signal from Sylvia, the Queen of the Night, now dressed in her magnificent, threatening costume, dagger in hand. I rested on her headdress while we moved center stage.

The conductor paused for the audience's laughter to fade before lifting his baton. At the first note, we were connected in the vengeful, explosive rage of the queen. My notes echoed and enhanced Sylvia's range. Our performance was exact and intense.

When the queen and I turned to leave the stage, the applause, the bravas, and tweets were thunderous.

As we waited for the final curtain call, I asked Sofia to explain the story behind the opera. She quickly obliged. "There are many messages within this opera. It's about choices, about bravery and friendship. To me, its essence illustrates a transition from foolishness to wisdom, from fearfulness to confidence."

When we stepped centerstage for a final bow, the audience renewed its approval. Soaking amid the accolades, I appreciated the parallel to my own story. My life's journey has been filled with fear and confusion. On my dear friend's advice, I listened to my heart song, to my true calling, which gave me the chance to fulfill my dreams. Brava, Mariel.

THE END

Author's Note

The Magic Flute struck me as an imaginative mix of fairy-tale adventure and comedy. Written in 1791, it was Mozart's last opera. The story is about compassion and inner strength. One of its most memorable characters is the Queen of the Night. Her brilliant, high-flying music makes her instantly iconic—especially the famous "Queen of the Night aria," whose blazing F6, bird-like coloratura high notes have made it one of the most recognizable pieces in all of opera. My own sense of her character was shaped in part by Diana Damrau's performance on YouTube, which is easy to find through Bing Videos.

Mockingbirds and cardinals can be very territorial. Although a fanciful story, I tried to use scenarios that ease the tension between them: when territorial lines relax in the winter, when food is plentiful, when a predator is near, or when they gather around a neutral space like the waterhole.

Murder of Crows

Exhausted after a harrowing flight from Dallas and soaked from a late-night thunderstorm, I decided to check in at police headquarters. Dripping wet, I greeted the bleary-eyed night owls who had the dusk-to-dawn duty. They rarely spoke but always acknowledged my arrival with a nod or a hoot. Making my way upstairs, I felt small comfort in seeing the hole I called an office.

My door was always open. That wasn't part of any worker-friendly policy; just that stacks of unsolved case files overflowed into the hallway, blocking the door. City lights twinkled in the distance, offering enough light to make my way around the reams of paperwork. Drat! Candy wrappers littered my desk. Those damn squirrels downstairs were using my space again. I could only hope for better accommodations when the new branch opened this Spring. Right now, I need a Texas gully-washer to do some housekeeping for me.

Time to visit the night-shift officers. I had one or two birdbrains on my team, but most were capable investigators. Russell, my sergeant, was a tough old coot who spent his career working homicide. He wasn't a high-flyer, but he had a keen sense of right and wrong. And he was good at his job. As I perched on the edge of his desk, he got a caw. At this late hour, that usually meant trouble.

Minutes later, Russell and I arrived at the edge of the heavily wooded city park. The steady downpour and a flickering streetlight offered little help in sorting out the scene. We examined the sweet young thing lying motionless in the middle of the well-worn path that stretched the length of the park. Who was she? How did she die? Why was she here? Was it accidental or intentional? I needed answers.

Russell pointed to the tire tracks across her sleek, lifeless body as I watched raven-colored quills drift into a nearby ditch. Must have been something heavy. Likely hit and run. As we surveyed the dark landscape, Russell spied a second feathered body deep in the rain-soaked weeds. Yes, tonight we had a murder of crows. I needed coffee.

After two hours of waiting, a sliver of sunlight signaled the end of the midnight storm and the arrival of the forensics team – more like a forensics pair, an MD named Tom and his no-name sidekick. Tom, a seasoned crime scene investigator with a taste for tragedy, waved as he approached. One of the local cops lifted the crime scene tape, deferring to Tom's gruff manner and imposing figure – large frame, heavy jowls, and dark, piercing eyes. His sidekick hefted the tools of their trade.

When Tom joined Russell and me beside the tire-marked body, he handed me a small bag. "Here you go, Hawkeye."

Even though it was a routine we had established in our early years together, the satisfaction of this small gesture never diminished. Neither did my desire for coffee. Quickly, I opened the sack and chucked down my first coffee bean of the day. I liked them raw and one at a time. It was an acquired taste, like working homicide.

Tom squatted to examine the wounds on the first victim as I turned to Russell. Who, how, and why thoughts raced through my head. "Besides two dead bodies, what do we know? Any witnesses? How about who called it in?"

Russell hesitated. "I think we have a witness. Well, maybe not an eyewitness. He's a petty thief that we've dealt with before; goes by Snake. He says he spoke to this young bird right before she died. Do you want to talk to him here or at the station?"

"Bring him here. Let's do it now before those vultures who call themselves reporters show up. And tell the locals to get rid of that gaggle of onlookers. They display no concern for the living but show up with a morbid curiosity for the dead and dying. I hate that."

A tough flight, a sleepless night, and two dead bodies added up to a rough day ahead. Hoping for a sorely needed energy boost, I popped another coffee bean. As the caffeine buzz grew stronger, I watched Russell yank the skinny small-time hood from the departing crowd and push him my way.

This guy didn't want to make eye contact, but I insisted. "Look at me, Snake. You might be our only witness. Or you could be our only suspect. I need to know what you know. Talk to me now, and maybe you can slither back under that rock you call home."

He decided to talk.

"Okay, okay. Like I was telling your sergeant, her name is Flora. And that pile of feathers in the weeds is her boyfriend, Chi. They're always together. Anyway, I don't know about him, but I heard Flora scream. It was raining hard, and by the time I got to her, she was barely breathing. Her eyes were closed, but she managed to whisper one word."

Snake paused. What's with this lizard? My blood pressure was climbing. "Okay, drama queen, I'll bite. What did she whisper?"

"My hearing's not so good, but it sounded like 'Nevermore.'"

I stumbled backward as I shouted. "You've got to be kidding! What kind of birdbrain quotes poetry as a dying declaration? Get out of here. And go get your ear buds cleaned."

Snake seemed anxious to oblige, but my sleep-deprived, caffeine-charged rant wasn't finished.

"And don't leave town. You're still on my radar. Go, before I change my mind."

After Snake skittered away, Russell poked at me. "Hawkeye, maybe he's right. If they were lovers, it's possible her last thoughts were about Chi – about losing him. Think about it."

Trying to ignore him, I turned to Tom for an update, but Russell persisted. "I'm not finished. Quit popping those coffee beans. They're not helping. You're jittery and not thinking squarely. You need to rest. I don't care where - just get some shut-eye. I'll check with forensics and then find us some breakfast. Be back in an hour." Then he was gone.

It's hard to do a self-assessment in the middle of a meltdown, but he was right. My heart was racing, and my thinking was muddled. The hundred-year-old red oak shrouding the crime scene had my name on it. I needed sleep.

Hasty decisions often lead to negative consequences. My snap choice to doze near the crime scene provided welcome relief for my weary body. But – there's always a but - I woke up to what looked like the mouths of hungry chicks, ten microphones begging for attention. No way to escape. And so, the questions began.

"Detective, are you okay? How do you feel? Can you tell us what happened? Who is the victim? Was it an accident? Was it gang-related? Why were you sleeping? Did you pass out? Are you injured?"

I pushed the microphones away, swearing to myself that if one more reporter asked me how I felt, I would rip their heart out. How I felt didn't matter, but my next steps did.

Pushing my way through the gauntlet of questions, I told them, "Dead is dead. Two bodies, no answers. I'll get back to you." I left them to gnaw on those slim pickings.

Thankfully, there was one important question they didn't ask, and one I forgot to pursue. Who reported it? Snake wasn't the answer. Then who? Witness, accomplice, or murderer; I needed to find out.

Feeling refreshed and clear-headed, I caught up with Tom and no-name as they prepared the bodies for the trip to the morgue. Their preliminary investigation must be complete. I shouted at Tom. "What have you found?"

"Glad you're back among the living. Your sergeant should return any minute with donuts. As for the victims, one scenario fits. They had to be close, perhaps embracing. The boyfriend took a direct hit from an unknown vehicle. That sent him sailing into the thistle. With no time to react, she was crushed by whatever rolled over her. Heavy rain washed away most of the evidence, except for a few remaining tire tracks. Not sure if they'll be much help. Oh, I have a surprise for you."

I yawned and waited. Yet another drama queen. There was no good reason to aggravate my esteemed teammate. Instead, I begged for an explanation, "Prey tell."

My dark humor wasn't lost on the good doctor. He chuckled, then said, "They weren't hit last night. It had to be 20 to 24 hours ago. Rough guess, mid-morning yesterday."

"Doc, that doesn't line up with our witness account. Snake said he heard Flora scream last night just before he found her."

Tom shrugged his shoulders. "I'm just telling you what the science says."

Still stunned by Tom's revelation, I didn't notice Russell's return until he shoved a French cruller in my face. "Hawkeye, maybe Snake didn't hear Flora? What if the scream came from our mysterious caller?"

God, I thought, maybe I should give up coffee beans. I quickly discounted that idea. Beans or no beans, Russell was on to something. I decided to test his recall.

"Think, Russell, what exactly did the caller say?"

Before he could answer, one of the officers guarding the crime scene interrupted. "Excuse me, detective. This little lady needs to speak to you. Says it's urgent."

Without waiting for agreement, a tiny, blue-coated thing introduced herself. "My name is Betty Lou Byrd. I live at the south end of the park, but we're moving two streets north – lots more room." She pointed over my shoulder, then continued. "Last night I was returning from a late meeting with our contractor. As I flew through here, I saw this poor, dead thing in the short grass; nobody else was around. All I could do was scream and hightail it home to call you folks."

I smiled. We had our mystery caller. "Thank you. You did the right thing. If you think of anything else, please let us know. Russell, give the lady a jelly donut and help her on her way."

Before a crumb touched her lips, Betty Lou shouted, "Wait, there is something else. This path has been overgrown for weeks, until three days ago. Someone's been mowing the grass. I don't know about you, but I think that could be dangerous."

I wanted to hug Betty Lou Byrd. Instead, I waited until she left, then hugged my sergeant. "Russell, I know what Flora tried to tell Snake. Remember, he admitted his hearing was bad. It wasn't nevermore. She was trying to warn him. I think she said new mower."

An odd look of disappointment crossed Russell's face; perhaps he had a romantic heart.

Unfortunately, my joy was tempered by a sad reality. Even if the crime guys could help us find the vehicle, there was little we could do. I decided to create a new file for hit-and-runs like this one. They don't belong in the Closed pile or the Unsolved stack. I need one labeled Unpunished.

"Get the public safety guys to put out the word. Folks need to know about the mowers in the park. Maybe we can avoid more incidents."

After a restless night dreaming about the doomed lovers, Flora and Chi, I made my way to the office. My early-bird sergeant leaned against my door frame. Doesn't this guy ever go home?

"What? Another case already."

Russell grinned. "No, boss. But we may have trouble; there are rumblings of a conspiracy. It's the Ravens, that gang that hangs out by the city reservoir. Apparently, they're talking to other neighborhood gangs. They're threatening to dive bomb and lay it on any lawn mowers that come through the city park. What should we do?"

I paused to take a deep breath—my turn to be a drama queen. "Wish them Godspeed."

THE END

Hattie and Whisper

Trying to conceal the bright orange spots that dotted my dark body, I nestled deep into the vivid green, heart-shaped leaves I called home. Slow-moving and leaf-bound, I longed for the moment when I could be free of my family. They spent their days eating pipevine leaves, talking about eating them, then crunching, munching, and eating some more. Pipevines, that's all their tiny brains were wired for. I wanted more.

One evening, a mysterious sound drifted through the garden, unlike the threat of bird calls or the rapid beat of wasp wings. It was mellow and soothing with the scent of jasmine carried on an ocean breeze. Every night, I waited—listening, hoping to hear that tender melody again.

My family didn't understand. Anything that didn't involve eating pipevines was uncaterpillary, a waste of time. Their bit of encouragement was to stop listening, stop dreaming, and start eating.

This morning, something scary and spectacular happened. I had seen the giant before. It often arrived with the morning sun, moving quietly through the garden, fussing over every flower. I decided to name it Whisper.

My short legs were great for crawling, not great for standing like Whisper. My body was long and spikey. I wanted to be tall and slender like the giant. Grasping the pipevine trellis to hoist myself upright, I teetered back and forth, swaying wildly until I tumbled to the ground. "Ouch!" There really is safety in numbers, all sixteen of them.

Whisper must have seen my nosedive. As I scooted up the pipevine, the giant approached, now nose to caterpillar. Although Whisper often talked to me, nothing made sense. Today was different. Among the giant's mumblings, I heard a sound I understood—just one word. "Cello."

Stunned, I realized that I could repeat it. That one sound, one word, opened a magical connection between our worlds, between caterpillar and giant. I looked into Whisper's dark eyes and shouted in my best caterpillar voice, "Cello!"

Whisper stumbled backward over pipevines, trampling bee balms and milkweeds. She quickly stood up, stared at me for several seconds, then ran from the garden.

"Oh, no. What have I done?" I pleaded for her to come back. "Stop, please!" My tears quickly evaporated in the warmth of the summer sun. Confused and hungry, I tried to understand what had happened. A nibble of pipevine satisfied the ache in my belly, but not the pain in my head and heart. What was this cello? Why did Whisper run?

Wishing desperately for answers, I decided to rest to clear my thoughts. As I curled up in the leafy shadows, my antennae twitched. These short appendages alerted me to changes in the air, whether an approaching storm or winged danger. It was neither wind nor wasp. It was the haunting melody. It was back.

Wide awake, I crawled to the edge of my leafy home. I wanted to find the source of this enchanting sound as it wafted through the pipevines. To my surprise, Whisper sat in front of the garden trellis. Her eyes were level with mine.

Staring at me, Whisper stroked a wand back and forth across an oddly shaped box. Here was the source of that magical sound. Whisper smiled and murmured one word, "Cello."

Mesmerized by the music, I couldn't move. Finally, a gush of words spewed from my mouth. "I named you Whisper. You can call me Hattie. I love the sound of this cello. Can we be friends?"

The giant smiled and nodded. "I like the name, Whisper. And yes, I'd like to be your friend."

Every day, Whisper ran to the garden to chat with me. Our morning conversations were brief. A quick, "Hello, dear friend," then Whisper would hurry off to prepare for school. Our evenings together were more pleasant. After her meal and homework, Whisper came to the garden where she extended her hand. When I crawled aboard, she said my orange spines tickled her palm. She often giggled and called me her little porcupine.

It was my favorite place, stretched out atop Whisper's shoulder. I listened as she completed her homework or practiced music lessons. We were an unlikely duo, sharing a bond inspired by the love of music—a bond that blossomed into a friendship filled with language and laughter.

Tonight, instead of curling up on Whisper's shoulder, I clutched her hair like a rope, climbing from her shoulder to the top of her head. Perched there, I felt my body was changing. Risking a scold from Whisper, I yelled, "I'm hungry. Do you have any pipevine stew or juicy green salad?"

Whisper put down her math book. "Hattie, pipevines are good for caterpillars but not for people. Hang on to my hair, and we'll check the pantry. Maybe we have something tasty you could eat."

Whisper's mama was busy dancing around the house with her new vacuum cleaner. She didn't seem to notice us poking through the pantry shelves. My sixteen legs marched in place as I anxiously waited for Whisper to complete her search. She shuffled through cans of veggies, bags of fruit, and packages of pasta before grabbing a box of cookies.

Whisper lifted a chunk of chocolate chip cookie to her head. "Taste this."

One bite was enough for me to know I wanted more. "Wow, these are yummy." I clamored from head to shoulder, leaving dandruff-like crumbs in Whisper's hair. I continued from shoulder to arm before crawling deep into the open cookie box.

Just then, Whisper's mama yelled, "Get out of the pantry. You've had your dinner."

Wham! I cringed as the pantry door slammed shut. Mama continued to yell at Whisper. "It's past your bedtime. Wash your face, brush your teeth, brush your hair, put on your jammies, and kiss your daddy goodnight."

As I listened to Mama's instructions, I imagined her finger pointing toward Whisper's bedroom. A "But Mama" cry from Whisper was quickly followed by "No buts, young lady," from Mama. Whisper huffed before I heard her footsteps running from the kitchen.

Hmmm, what to do? I'm trapped in the pantry surrounded by chocolate chip cookies, and my friend will be gone until morning. What to do? I sighed. Afterall, I am a caterpillar. I had to do what caterpillars did—eat.

Exhausted from all the munching and crunching, I curled up

next to a bag of lemons. After hours of tossing and turning, a scream jolted me awake. It was Whisper's mother. "Eek! There's a big, fat caterpillar in our pantry."

Mama clenched the pantry door and yelled for her daughter. "Get in here now and take this prickly pickle of a bug back to the garden. When Whisper arrived, still in her pajamas, she ducked under Mama's outstretched arm. I didn't have a chance to yell surprise before Whisper grabbed me and ran to the garden.

"Oh, Hattie, I'm so sorry you were stuck in the pantry all night."

"That's all right, Whisper. I ate a lot of cookies."

Whisper dropped me off on the trellis, said goodbye, then left to get ready for school. Alone again, I noticed my body had grown longer and wider. I overdid delicious. What if those cookies affect my transformation into a butterfly? What if my adult body is shaped like a cookie? What if my wings have chocolate chip spots instead of yellow ones? Worried about my future, I looked for a cozy place to hang out and think.

Whisper's family had just returned from a week-long vacation. As soon as Daddy unlocked the car doors, Whisper ran to greet her caterpillar friend. But Hattie was not daydreaming on the pipevine trellis. After inspecting every leaf, Whisper began again. Glassy-eyed, she hoped her friend was playing a game of hide-and-seek. After an hour of searching, Whisper panicked. "Hattie, I give up. Where are you? Please answer!"

Leaves rustled in the late-day breeze. No longer holding back tears, she hurried through the garden. "Oh no, oh no." What if she were eaten by a bird or stung by a wasp?

Exhausted from the search, Whisper ran into the house. When she told Mama that Hattie was missing, Mama tried to calm Whisper, "Maybe her family took a vacation too. It's time to get ready for bed. Hattie will probably be waiting for you tomorrow."

That didn't help. As she pulled her favorite green blanket under her chin. Closing her eyes, she pleaded for Hattie's return. "Please, please, please be safe, little friend." With that, she fell asleep.

Tap, tap, tap. Tap, tap, tap.

What? What was that sound? Was it a dream? Whisper rubbed her eyes.

Tap, tap, tap.

She checked the window—maybe hail from a midnight storm? No, the window was dry. She turned from the window. In the glow of her nightlight, she spied a tiny figure on her desk. Cautiously, Whisper slipped out of bed. She thought it looked like a hummingbird."

Tip-toeing closer, Whisper realized it wasn't a bird. "Am I dreaming? Are you a fairy?"

The tiny creature nodded. "My name is Dancer. Do you like my sparkly shoes? I just got them from the fairy cobbler. Dancing is part of my job. I do it to get attention. Listen."

Sleepy and confused, Whisper watched as the fairy danced on her desktop.

Tap, tap, tap. Tap, tap, tap. "Aren't they great? They have such a snappy sound."

Still sleepy, Whisper tried to be polite. "Your shoes are very nice. But why are you here? Why are you dancing on my desk?"

"Easy. I am here to give you a message from your caterpillar friend. While you were away, her body needed to change. She couldn't wait for you; her little body couldn't wait for you. Before caterpillars become butterflies, they must rest. They do this in a snug little hideaway called a chrysalis. Hattie asked me to tell you goodbye."

Tears filled Whisper's eyes. Sobbing, she asked, "Will I ever see my friend again?"

Dancer didn't answer. She sat quietly, staring at her shoes. At last, "Hattie asked me the same question as she tucked herself into her chrysalis. Her body had a lot of work to do as it converted from a long, crawly thing into a delicate flying thing."

Dancer explained that the bond between a caterpillar and a girl was unknown to fairies. They couldn't guess if Hattie would remember Whisper when she emerged as a butterfly. "Hattie may be lost to you forever. Or one day you might spy her flitting from flower to flower, enjoying the sweet springtime blossoms. Yes, it's sad to be forgotten, just remember that during your special time together, your differences didn't matter. You loved her like a sister, and she loved you like a caterpillar."

Whisper woke to a room filled with sunshine. She threw off the bedcovers and declared, "I have a plan." Quickly dressing, she called for her father. "Daddy, I need your help to build an airplane."

In a dark corner of the garden under a half-eaten milkweed leaf, I stirred to free myself from my snug cocoon. Shaking off the dampness of my newborn wings, I eased my way into the sunlight. I was born to fly. I wanted to travel, but first things first, I needed to eat.

After draining the nectar from a nearby honeysuckle blossom, I was ready to fly, to soar as high as my wings could carry me, riding on the glorious ocean breeze. No bags to pack, no family to kiss goodbye. I tested my flight readiness with a few lifts and landings. Yep, good to go.

The higher I rose, the more breathtaking the view. I relished my airborne freedom as I darted from flower to flower, sampling their luscious flavors. Exhausted from this first outing, I settled onto a familiar vine. Its musty taste stirred memories of my life as a caterpillar. Nothing made sense: strange sounds, unusual places, enormous dark eyes.

A short rest didn't clear the puzzling images, nor did it relieve my hunger. I spotted the purple blossoms of a bee balm plant. Settling on its colorful petals, I sipped the flower's sweetness. As I enjoyed this morning treat, my antennae twitched, not in a good way. Something wasn't right, but what?

I tucked my wings into the shadows of the bee balm. Motionless, I struggled to identify the sound. Like the approach of a thunderstorm, leaves swirled, flowers flew. I was thrown from my hiding place, landing upside-down on a nearby pipevine. Frightened but curious, I righted myself. Quietly stealing from leaf to leaf, I spied a huge contraption rolling through the garden.

Thud! The pipevine shuddered as the wooden heap crashed into the garden trellis.

Startled, I watched as a vaguely familiar giant emerged. It moved back and forth through the garden, its eyes scanning every flower. I gasped when the giant bent toward my hiding place.

In a soft voice, it spoke. "Cello, my sweet friend."

My heart raced, my memory stirred as the giant continued, "I am Whisper."

In that instant, I recognized my friend—the dark eyes, the music and laughter of my dreams. With one huge butterfly leap, I landed on Whisper's nose. Best friends together again. I bounced up and down with excitement, "Cello, Whisper, cello."

THE END

Talking to Spiders

Morning sunbeams danced through sheer lavender curtains as I dug furiously in the timothy hay that was both snack and bedding. Tears dampened the amber strands as they flew from my crate.

An unfamiliar voice interrupted the mayhem. "Why are you crying?"

Startled, I tumbled backwards. My best friend Sofia, a ten-year-old girl, should be at school. The house ought to be empty. Motionless, I scanned my surroundings. "Who said that? Where are you?"

"It's me, Sabio, here above your food dish."

Squinting, I connected the voice with a slender eight-legged body dangling inside her crate. "I've seen you before, but you never speak."

"True, but I always listen. When I heard you sobbing, I knew it was time."

"I've cried before, and you never spoke. Why now?"

Sabio hesitated. "I sensed a deep grief that requires more than a tantrum to satisfy."

Agitated, I challenged him. "You're a spider. What do you know about grief?"

Sabio lowered himself to the food dish. "Most spiders live as phantoms, unknown to the rest of the world. Yet, when seen, it is often our fate to be trampled. It is a matter of survival that keeps us hidden. Until recently, you and your friend were always planning adventures, reading, dancing, and laughing. Not now."

Abby burst into tears. "Yes, my friend is always angry. After school, she yells at her family. Then she runs in here and yells at me. Even worse—no cuddles. I feel like a rabbit, no longer a friend, and I don't understand why."

Sabio's eight eyes focused on my own. "The answers aren't buried in your hay. We need to dig into your friend's anger. Once we root out the cause, we can try to restore her happiness."

Still doubting this eight-legged Freud, I suggested we chat somewhere cozy. Rattling the crate door, I proposed we meet under the bed. "First, can you help me get out of this locked crate?"

"Hold out your paw." I extended my front foot and watched Sabio weave silk threads between paw and latch. Finally, "Okay, I want you to pull, slowly, very slowly."

The latch lifted as I tugged the silky rope. The crate door clanked open. I couldn't believe it. "Wow, this is great." Shaking off the webbing, I scurried under the bed.

Sabio swung from the crate to the bedpost. "Tell me everything."

"Last month, my friend came home with a nasty scratch on her arm. When I asked what had happened, she said she had fallen into a rosebush. Then she said a strange thing. 'Don't tell Mama.'"

Sabio crossed two of his legs. "Why is that strange?"

Clearing my throat, I explained, "You know that my friend and I can talk to each other. The rest of her family only hears bunny noises. Why would she say, 'Don't tell Mama,' when she knows I can't talk to her mother?"

Sabio nodded thoughtfully.

"And last week, I heard her arguing with her mother about a jacket. Afterward, she ran in here, slammed the door, burst into tears, and buried herself under the bedcovers. When I hopped on the bed to snuggle, she pushed me away."

"How distressing for both of you."

"Yes, I thought I was her best friend, but now I'm just a caged rabbit whose bond with a special friend is broken. I don't know how to fix it."

Sabio hesitated, then whispered. "We need help."

The afternoon ticked away while we remained hidden under the bed. When family voices interrupted our thoughts, I hurried into my crate. "Oh no, what about the door? We don't have time for another rope trick."

Sabio returned to the top of the crate. "Maybe she won't notice."

I shuddered when the bedroom door slammed shut. Sofia dropped her backpack and pounced onto the bed. I could hear her sobbing in her favorite pillow.

Abby crept onto Sofia's bed. She tugged at a strand of brown hair. No response. Next, she nudged Sofia's arm. With a big sniff, Sofia pulled Abby close. "My sweet Bun-Bun. I've been mean to you. I'm sorry. I'm a mess, and I don't know what to do."

Gently nudging my friend's cheek, I offered support. "I can help."

Through glassy eyes, Sofia offered a sad smile, "You're just a rabbit. What can you do?"

In a stern voice, Abby disagreed. "I am not just a rabbit. I am your friend. Don't we have lots of adventures? I'm not good at math, but I look great in my pirate outfit."

Sofia laughed. "Stop. Those things are true, but this is different. You don't understand."

In a cross voice, Abby poked at her friend. "Help me understand. Your happiness switch is broken. I want to fix it."

"I thought I had real friends, school friends. Now I don't know what to think." Abby watched as Sofia buried her head again. "You can't help. Please go back to your crate."

Sofia's nighttime routine included refilling Abby's water bottle, but tonight, without a word, Sofia crawled into bed. Teary-eyed, Abby mouthed goodnight to her unhappy friend. She dozed fitfully until Sabio tickled her nose.

"Wake up. My friends arranged for us to meet a pixie named Elida. She specializes in helping distressed creatures. She will be here at midnight."

The pair dozed as hours passed. A faint tapping signaled Elida's arrival. Abby stared at the hummingbird-sized fairy dancing across Sofia's scattered schoolbooks.

She watched as Elida turned to Sabio. "Thank you for reaching out to me. There are many cases like Sofia's. If we're going to help, we must work quickly." Waving her tiny wand, she swept shimmering green fairy dust over girl, rabbit, and spider.

Elida settled next to Sofia's ear. "May we come into your dream?"

Abby and Sabio waited beside Elida. Finally, a troubled voice answered. "It's dark in here."

"I know." As she spoke, a green glow surrounded Elida. "I travel with my own light. Join us. Your bunny and her spider pal are here. They are worried about you."

A surprised voice responded, "I didn't know my bunny had a spider pal. Spiders are scary."

Elida quickly responded. "Yes, like spiders, many things are scary; some deserve our fright, some deserve our understanding."

From the darkness, "Why are you in my dreams?"

Elida offered a simple answer. "To listen."

And there was a simple but testy reply. "Listen to what? My snoring?"

Abby chuckled, but Elida persisted. "No, dear, I'm here to listen to your sadness. You have isolated yourself. Your family, your bunny—they don't understand why you are unhappy.

That's spider-scary for them."

Sobbing from the darkness, "You don't understand. Spider-scary is easy. You just stomp on them. I feel trapped and don't know how to explain—not even to myself."

Before the pixie could stop him, Sabio broke in. "Hold on, I'm a spider. How do you think I feel? Stomping is easy unless you're the spider."

Elida pointed her wand at Sabio. "Shouting doesn't help." Elida turned to the darkness. "Let's try to understand ... together. Tell me what's going on."

Sofia shuffled in the shadows. Her voice sounded closer. "I thought I had a best friend at school. She encouraged me to share secrets, clothes, and food. Sharing—isn't that what friends do?"

Elida agreed. "Sharing is a part of friendship. So, what changed?"

Sofia sniffed and replied, "As we walked home after school, I told her I got an A on our math test. She called me a nerd, then pushed me into a thorny bush. Instead of helping me, she skipped away. She said it was an accident. My arms were scratched.

"Another day, she said she wanted a pair of shoes for her birthday. She knew I didn't get a big allowance. When I suggested another gift, she told everyone I was poor. She said, 'If you don't have money, then give me something you already have—like your new jacket.' I didn't want her friends to laugh at me, so I gave it to her."

The distraught voice continued. "She also took cookies from my lunchbox. Of course, I didn't stop her. She was hungry. But the next day, she ate my whole sandwich. I wanted to be a good friend, but I was hungry, too."

Sabio interrupted Sofia. "Wait, wait. That's not right. "Hiding in the dark can't change the truth. Shoving, demanding, taking—that's not sharing."

Elida rapped her tiny wand. "You're a pushy little bug, aren't you?"

Elida shushed a giggle from Abby. "Sabio is right. Friendship is more than sharing. It's about kindness and acceptance. It's time for you to come out of the shadows."

After a grand swoosh of Elida's wand, Abby and Sabio were standing off-stage in a shadowy theater. From behind heavy crimson curtains, they peered at an audience full of spiders.

Elida and a rabbit-sized Sofia stood center-stage. A large yellow and black spider dangled over the podium. "Welcome to the Biannual Garden Spider Conference. Tonight's topic is Recognizing Friends from Foes. Please welcome our friend Elida and our guest speaker, Sofia.

Elida fluttered over the microphone. "Friendship isn't always easy. Your enemies come in many forms. Sometimes it's a robin, and sometimes it's the smell of cinnamon." Oohs rippled through the audience.

"Sofia, a human, is struggling with her ability to recognize friends. Please keep an open mind and help me welcome her." Abby heard several grumbles above the faint applause.

As Sofia shuffled forward, she pleaded with Elida. "I can't speak to a bunch of spiders."

Elida drew Sofia to the microphone. "You have a voice, and

you have a story that needs to be told. These creatures rely on their ability to distinguish between friend and foe. For some, it's easy, but for many, it's difficult. Your struggle with friendship issues may help them."

"Spiders are scary. No, no, I can't do it."

"Remember, this is a dream. With one swoosh, I can swap your parents for the spiders."

Sofia shook her head. "Please, not my parents. I'll talk to the spiders."

Abby remained offstage, close to Sofia, while Sabio made his way to an empty seat.

Elida reassured Sofia. "Don't be afraid. Speak about your feelings."

Staring at Elida and loud enough to be overheard by the audience, "All I feel is afraid."

A spidery jeer came from behind Sabio. "How do you think I feel? You and I hide in the dark. You're afraid of friendship. I'm afraid of big feet."

Surprising everyone, Sofia walked to the edge of the stage. She looked taller. Sofia bent toward the taunting little spider, "We're both afraid and hiding in the darkness."

Sofia nodded toward Sabio, "Thankfully, someone reminded me that hiding doesn't change the truth."

Sofia explained. "Fear can protect you and warn you of danger. Or it can trap you. It can keep you from seeing and doing what's right. It can suck the happiness right out of you."

Sabio jumped to the back of his chair. "Wait, wait. Are you talking about darkness or friendship? Darkness isn't always a bad thing. I live most of my life in the dark."

"Sabio, you're right." Sofia nodded. "That kind of dark protects you. But for me, even in the sunshine, I felt dark inside where my feelings got all muddled. I've been so confused about my friendships that my world became a sad, angry, and lonely place."

On hearing this, Abby reached out to her friend. Before Elida shushed her away, Abby mumbled, "You're not alone."

Sofia smiled and turned to Elida. "My bunny is right. I'm not alone. I have her and a great family. The hard part is admitting I made a friendship mistake."

Suddenly, a small spider skittered toward Sofia, waving several bright orange legs. "What mistake are you talking about? In our world, a mistake can mean life or death. We don't get many second chances. Sounds like you do."

Sofia stood motionless, her mouth open without words. The audience froze. Sofia's body was changing. Her arms and legs were longer, her body bigger. With both hands over her heart, she bowed toward the audience. In a soft voice, she apologized. "I'm sorry. I didn't think . . ."

Waving its legs, the spider interrupted again. Abby chuckled, "This feisty little critter isn't giving up."

The spider continued, "You didn't think. It's easier not to think, not to care, easier to stomp without considering the consequences. I don't want to be mush on your shoe!"

With applause from the audience, Sofia bowed again and retreated from the stage.

In a harsh voice, Sofia confronted Elida. "When you brought me to speak at this conference, you said I could help them discover friend from foe. I didn't do that. These spiders are a scary bunch, and they know about fear." She paused. "I didn't help them; they helped me."

Sabio climbed onto Abby's back as they listened to Sofia. "I was afraid of losing a friend I never had. She stomped on me without thinking of the consequences to me. And I let her do it. I didn't stand up for myself." She gently stroked Abby's ears, "The more I hid the confusion and hurt inside me, the darker it got and the smaller I felt. Hiding those feelings didn't make them go away."

Everyone watched as the spider audience faded in the soft glow of dawn. Elida turned to Sofia. "When you wake, you might remember talking to spiders. And you will recognize your real friends, those who love you."

It was Sabio's turn. "Don't be spider mush on someone else's shoe."

With a swoosh of fairy dust, Abby heard Elida whisper, "Time to wake up, friends."

Feeling the warmth of the morning sun, Abby stretched and watched as her silent friend, Sabio, added a silvery strand to his web. When Sofia's alarm sounded, Abby bounded onto the bed. After a toothy yawn, Sofia pulled Abby close, "Good morning, Bun-Bun."

"Good morning, Sleepyhead. No school today. What's the

plan?"

Abby moaned when Sofia held up three fingers. "I hope one is an adventure."

Sofia held up her thumb. "Number one: Yesterday, Mama asked me to clean my messy closet. I want to surprise her."

Abby frowned. "I like your mother, but that doesn't sound like an adventure."

"Two, I've decided to find new friends."

"Maybe we can find them in the closet." Abby touched Sofia's nose. "What's number three?"

"I need to tell Mama how I lost my jacket. She might be angry, but I need to tell her the truth. Will you come with me?"

"Of course, Sofia. What are friends for?"

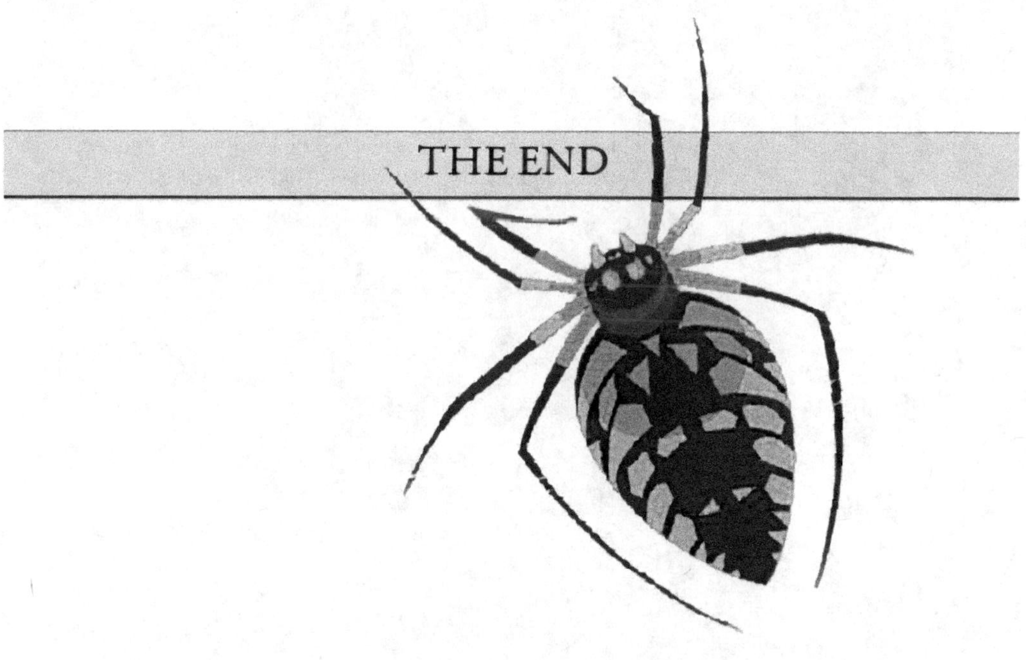

Tossed and Found

"I've seen a lot of crap, Gram."

Her silver hair framed a weathered face, her graying eyes still twinkled with childlike impishness, and her gentle hand warmed me like an angel's caress. Gram nodded. "I'm sure you have, sweet thing. Tell me about it."

She stroked my head and waited. I considered whether retracing my journey would rekindle past pain or release me from it. It was time. Squirming closer to her side, I began.

"It was a stormy night, but not a Mother Nature kind of gale. This bitter storm raged inside a small, wood-framed ranch house. The thunder of angry voices, a brutish hand around my neck, I knew my fate was writ when I was stuffed into a dark plastic bag. Barking, growling, pleading for mercy, all useless. I wanted to live. I just needed to figure out how."

Gram patted my shoulder. "You're a fighter, aren't you?"

Without reply, I continued. "It happened quickly—the speeding car, the sound of rushing air, the bone-crushing landing. Looking back, it was a small blessing to land on a clump of muhly grass rather than on unforgiving pavement.

With a broken leg and barely enough air to breathe, my teeth tore furiously through the plastic shroud meant to be my coffin. Bundled like garbage, discarded like trash, I squeezed myself through a ragged hole, a rebirth of sorts, into the moonless night. Although racked with pain, I managed a bloody smile, then out loud I yelped, "Tomorrow I may live or die—either way, I am free."

A teardrop dampened the scruff of my neck as Gram stretched for the tissue box, never far from her nose. After a honk like the call of a migrating goose, she sniffed and whispered. "The pain of rejection can linger long after the ache of broken bones. It can torture the soul." For a fleeting moment, I wondered what secret agony hid in her aging body.

"Yes, Gram, except for the rousing warmth of the morning sun, I would have surrendered to my predicament. Awake and squinting into the daylight, I assessed my wounds: my left eye swollen shut, my front leg crippled, my body cloaked in bruises. As I scanned my surroundings, my gaze was drawn to a welcome whiff of food drifting on the breeze. Luckily, my undamaged nose guided me toward a nearby drainage ditch, hopping and hoping for breakfast. A paper sack tangled in roadside brambles offered a few stale breadcrumbs."

Gram slowly stroked my side, as if counting each rib. "That doesn't sound like much food."

"You're right. It wasn't enough to satisfy my hunger. Oddly, the nightmarish ordeal made me appreciate those few morsels more than any tasty bowl of canned food. Afterward, I stretched out in the sunshine to warm my aching bones. My bulging left eye was worthless, probably crushed when I hit the ground. The right eye slowly focused on an end-row building, its brick wall splashed with paint. Intrigued, wounds forgotten, I pulled myself out of the ditch and hobbled forward.

Hunger and pain aside, I sat mesmerized by colors I'd never seen, colors that changed in the shadows of passing clouds, colors that stirred my imagination. Unfortunately, something else stirred—the pain in my left side. I needed a place to rest, perhaps a place to die. Trembling and with no shelter in sight, I struggled to dig a shallow bed at the base of the wall."

Gram pulled me into her lap. "Did you dream?"

Staring into her eyes, I mused, "An odd question, Gram. I guess I slept fitfully, for hours or days; I'm not sure. My thoughts and, yes, my dreams fixed on that wall, on the mingling of light and dark, on the freedom with which each color danced across that hard surface. I remember waking to a cold downpour. Struggling to move and with nowhere to go, I decided to stay close to the wall; its bold colors warmed my spirit, if not my rain-soaked fur.

"By morning, mud-caked, hungry, and hurting, I tried to stand. Not good. Yelping, I fell back against the wall. That's when I heard voices. Fearful and unable to walk, I waited and listened.

"Two voices approached. 'Let's see how it held up in the storm.' As they rounded the corner, both stopped and stared. I was hoping their gaze was on the wall. The freckle-faced gal lifted her hand to stop the approach of her auburn-haired friend. In a harsh voice, 'Wait, Misha, I think it's a rat. Don't get too close. What if it has rabies?'

“Misha pushed her friend’s hand aside. ‘Don’t be silly, Becky. It’s a chihuahua. That’s why it’s so small.’ She continued to talk, her voice soothing, as she reached out. ‘Hey, sweet thing, what happened to you? How about a bath and some food? Oh my, your eye looks bad.’ I barked when she touched my damaged leg. ‘You poor thing. Let’s get you to a vet.’

“The wall seemed to be Becky’s focus. ‘Misha, what about our artwork? The street festival is next week. I don’t see any storm damage, but it needs some finishing touches. Why don’t you get that ratty thing to the vet, and I’ll finish our mural?’

“Misha agreed. ‘Thanks, Becky. Don’t forget to sign it.’ I whimpered in pain as she lifted me to eye level and asked, ‘What shall I call you?’

“Mocking my size and appearance, Becky chuckled, ‘How about Tinkerbell?’ Both girls laughed before Misha disagreed. ‘No, maybe something shorter. Tink it is. Let’s get you some help.’

“My memory of the vet is hazy - warm bath, flashes of color, masked faces. I woke up groggy and alone in a small wire cage, my neck bound with a collar so big I couldn’t see the rest of me. Although my pain was gone, a different loss overshadowed that welcome news. I was trapped; my freedom was stolen once more. If dogs could cry … I begged the universe to set me free.”

I heard Gram laugh quietly. “It sent my granddaughter instead.”

“Yes, it did.” We both laughed. “Gram, I could use a snack.”

Always accommodating, she agreed. "Sure, chewy or crunchy? I'll top off my coffee."

"Yes, please, to both."

From the time Misha introduced us, her grandmother and I have had a magical connection. At our first meeting, she sat in a yellow-cushioned rocker, book in hand, a blue pen stuck over her left ear. Setting the book aside, she leaned toward me and stared, her two blue-gray eyes to my single dark one, then whispered, "Come here, sweet thing." I hobbled forward, a black patch over a worthless eyeball and a pink cast bracing my left leg. When she lifted me to her lap, like super-glue, we bonded. From that time forward, she has been my confidant, my sage, my voice, and interpreter of all things human.

When Gram returned from the kitchen, hot coffee and treats in hand, I hopped into her lap and quickly snapped up a crunchy biscuit. "Where were we?"

After a loud slurp of caffeine, Gram replied. "I think we're at the point where Misha brings you home from the hospital."

"Right. Confined again, I freaked out during the car ride home—to many terrifying flashbacks. I pawed, I gnawed, I trembled and whined for the entire trip. I didn't calm down until Misha pulled me from that soft-sided prison she called a pet carrier and put me in front of you, announcing, 'Meet Tink.'"

I stretched my body as Gram swept her warm hand across my back. "My apologies for laughing at your name. Misha explained its origin, and I had to agree."

She chuckled, "Yes, your freedom came at a high price, but it opened a new kind of independence, one of self-determination. When I first looked into your sad little eye, I saw flashes of color, flames of a creative soul—an artist waiting for inspiration."

I pressed my paw on her wrinkled hand. "Thanks, Gram." After a bite of my blueberry-flavored chew, I continued. "But I didn't see flames in your eyes. I saw a tunnel, swirling with brilliant colors, inviting yet frightening, pulling me forward into your world."

Gram sighed, "Yes, in that instant our worlds collided, our souls, our destiny forever entangled. Now tell me about your art."

That's quite a leap, Gram, from your eyes to my art."

Gram chuckled, "Yes, it is. I can recite Misha's stories from the time she could lift a crayon. Her techie job only helped her achieve her dream of owning an art gallery. I know her art history. Continue with yours."

After a long sigh, "My painful recovery took three months but offered a few surprise benefits. Misha kept me close, handfeeding me and tending to my injuries. Best of all, she tucked me inside her jacket as we toured art museums, galleries, libraries, and murals around town, educating ourselves as we went.

Over time, I developed an abstract style that Misha described as canine Jackson Pollock. Lots of bold tail-strokes, usually after breakfast when I had lots of energy. My bedtime art tended to be sweeping and rhythmic like a queen's wave. And I always signed my work with a pink swoosh.

When I appeared in public, people adored my uniqueness, a black patch over one eye and a pink binding over my gimpy leg. One gallery visitor declared 'Aww, what a cute little pirate.'

From then on, people asked about the Pink Pirate. Everyone, especially me, loved the name.

Gram patted my head. "Names don't usually change, but nicknames adapt to character. My birth name is Sofia, but now everyone calls me Gram. Tink suited you at the time of your rescue. Now you are the Pink Pirate, resourceful, daring, and colorful."

I nodded agreement, "Yes, the nickname fits."

Thoughtfully, I explained. "I literally stepped into art. Most evenings, Misha laid several canvases on the floor with jars of paint and trays of brushes scattered around them. From my cozy bed, I studied her color choices and brush techniques.

"One late night, Misha knelt before a primed canvas, the usual clutter of paints and brushes nearby. In a hurry to get to the doggie door, I figured the shortest path to relief lay between the canvas and Misha. In my haste, I stepped from her mixing tray onto the canvas. Trying to shake off midnight blue, I knocked over two jars: teal and lemon-yellow. Slipping, sliding, mixing colors with my butt, I skidded across the canvas. Shrieking, Misha grabbed me and raced to the sink. After a scrub and a scolding, we returned to the canvas. Misha stuffed me in her oversized smock pocket and stared at the chaos of colors. She smiled, then said, 'I like it! Let's try another.'

"What began as an accident lit the fire that was my calling. Misha and I loved painting together. At first, people saw me only as her "save-the-animals" project, a one-eyed, limping dog. My art exposed them to the true dog inside, to the creativity that was my heart and soul.

"After years of murals, street fairs, and party sketches, Misha resigned from her techie job and bought a studio to display our work as well as that of other artists. I barked constantly on our road trip to the new location. When she lifted me from the car, I was stunned. Before me stood a solid brick building with a faded, yet familiar, mural on its west wall. A sad homecoming. I suppose fate is the artist.

"As Misha lifted me out of the car, she asked, 'What do you think?' I hopped out of her arms, trotted to the wall, and peed on it."

Gram chuckled. "A strange baptism, indeed."

"For weeks, Misha struggled to name her new studio, names like The Barking Brush and Pawsitive Art. When she suggested Tossed and Found, a tribute to my journey, I barked agreement. Misha gathered me in her arms, and together we danced. The choice was made.

"At our opening gala, I wandered through the crowded gallery, accepting pats on my head. Small crowds would gather to remark on tail-strokes, color, and composition. My signature piece hung in the entryway. Misha labeled it *First Steps* because I trotted all over the canvas, mixing colors as I raced for the doggie door. I called it *Relief*.

Our masterwork had stormy grays, dark blues, ominous black with red splotches meant to be teeth marks. No tail-work, only paws and claws digging a hole through the canvas. Misha titled it *Rage*; I called it *Rebirth*. Another canvas filled with streaks of every shade of blue completed my contribution to the show. Misha labeled it *Rain*; I called it *Tears*. Amazing how the same image evokes such different reactions. Isn't that the power of abstract art?"

Gram nodded and said, "Truly."

"I don't have enough paws to count the dog years since Misha rescued me. The early ones were filled with pain, the middle years with art and accolades, and my senior years with love and reflection. Throw in several dog biscuits along the way, and I've had a good run. Funny how the brain doesn't seem to recognize the passage of time the way the body does. It's been a joyful and art-filled life. Sadly, my vet recently declared I have a failing heart. I'm dying, Gram.

"Now, I want to end my life with dignity. Your granddaughter is talented and sentimental. She has given me a wonderful life and does not want to let me go. I love her for that, but prolonging my stay means enduring the bittersweet pain of living. I need your help. Will you tell her it's time for me to go? Will you stay with me when I die?"

Gram hesitated, then pulled me close. "Yes, sweet thing, I will look into your eye and watch the brilliant colors you love draw you, once again, into a miraculous new world."

"I'm ready, Gram."

THE END

FACE TO THE RAIN CITATIONS

Face to the Rain

Image rendered by Microsoft AI, Copilot Jack, p. 7
Image by Photorama from Pixabay, p. 8
Image by Anna Grzonka from Pixabay, p. 9, 10
Image by JayMantri from Pixabay, pp. 12-13
Image by Felix-Mittermeier from Pixabay, p. 14
Image by NoName_13 from Pixabay, p. 15
Image by Leo from Pixabay, pp. 16-17
Photo by KI Sutphin, p. 18
Image by Gregor Mima from Pixabay, p. 20
Composite Image by Reiner Rodenwald and John from Pixabay p. 21
Image by wasi1370 from Pixabay, p. 22
Image by Miguel Angel Fernández Romero from Pixabay, p. 23
Image by Tina from Pixabay, pp. 24-25
Photo by KI Sutphin, p. 25
Image by Tung Lam from Pixabay, pp. 26-27
Boonyachoat image from www.istockphoto.com, pp. 28-29
Image by ED WORKS from Pixabay, pp. 30-31
Image by G Halpin from Pixabay, p. 32
MS Copilot Jack generated image, pp. 33, 36, 38, 40, 41, 42
Image by Mabel Amber, who will one day from Pixabay, p. 46
Divider Image by Cyril from Pixabay, pp. 48, 50, 52
Photo by KI Sutphin, p. 55
AI generated image, pp. 56, 59, 61, 63
Image by Driss Chaoui, pp. 66, 67, 68, 70, 74, 76
Composite Image by Myléne from Pixabay and AI Copilot Jack, p. 78
Image by Myléne from Pixabay, pp. 79, 80, 82, 84, 86
Photo by KI Sutphin, p. 88

For more youthful stories, click the QR code below to visit Abby's Adventures Series.

AWI - adventure writers ink & Station WIL

THE SKY BETWEEN US:

And the Voices That Bind Us

Three Sisters ||| *Three Voices*

The Storied Trail

by CS Norwood

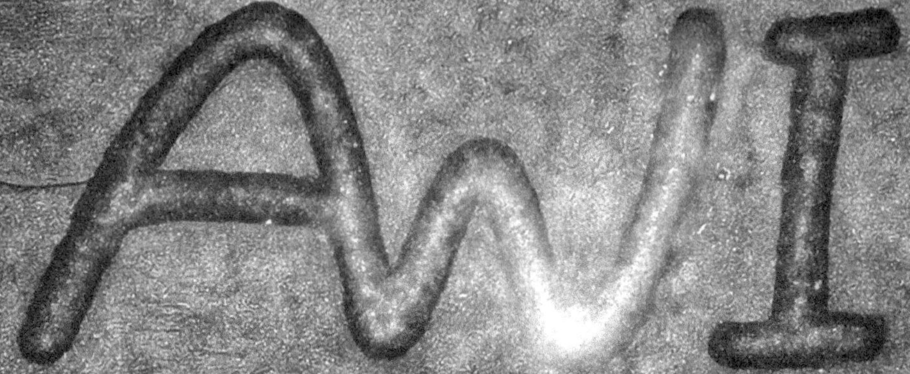

OLD BRANDS

A few stories from 30 years ago ...

The Storied Trail

by CS Norwood

A TEXAS STORY

The flat light of midafternoon washed the solitary lavender-clad figure almost as pale as the bleached brown dust she stood in. A lone crow cawed from his perch in the mesquite thicket at the end of the draw as two red and white speckled longhorns across the roadway stepped forward in unison, heads bowed as they cropped the sparse, dry blades of grass. None of them, however, seemed mindful of the old woman who endured the silence and tolerated the air of indifference in her usual manner. She stood with her head held unnaturally high, looking neither right nor left, but with eyes focused straight ahead on what may have been some far-off thought. Even the powerful Texas-sized jackrabbit that hopped in slow motion, kangaroo style, not ten feet from her side paid her any notion. In a world of butterflies, lazy buzzing bees, jackrabbits and longhorn cattle, Violet Sheldon stood alone and virtually colorless.

"It's about damn time," she mumbled flatly, as first the drone of the powerful engine and then the silver dome of the Greyhound topped the rise. She bent her knees and retrieved the blue flower-covered valise at her side as the bus slid to a stop in front of her, stirring a cloud of dust to accompany the noisy hiss and metallic squeak of air brakes and automatic doors.

As Violet gave herself up to the sleek beast, not even the jackrabbit poised motionless in the dry thistle took notice.

"Pardon me, is this seat taken?"

A slight blonde teenager in blue jeans and jacket, appearing to be wired directly into a yellow Walkman radio, lifted her eyes rather blankly at Violet's question, then cast scornfully about at the dozen or so empty seats surrounding them. She shrugged her angular shoulders, focused straight through Violet's eye sockets, and pinpointed somewhere on the other side of her skull.

"Be my guest, lady," she clipped, and turned her head to stare at the blur of the roadside. At once the girl resumed her head bobbing and chin jutting that Violet assumed coincided with the musical rhythm emanating from the Walkman.

Violet Sheldon seated herself beside the silent, undulating girl and was, again, alone in the world.

"Dammit!"

The sudden expletive jarred Violet's sweaty half-sleep. She moved her sore neck slowly and wiped the drool from the corner of her mouth. The highway sped by as she collected herself.

"Damn…lady, ya got any triple A's in that purse a yers?" The teen drawled as she mashed buttons and snapped tiny compartments on the radio.

"I'm not accustomed to carrying 'triple A's' with me." Violet retorted as she smoothed some invisible creases on her dress.

"Well, that cuts it!" Teen snapped as she yanked the headset from her ears. Violet wondered how long this young girl would survive disconnected from what seemed to be her life support system. "What'm I gonna do for the rest of this bor-ing trip!?" The girl flung her head back onto the black vinyl of the seat in a gesture of total dejection.

"Well, we could talk…" Violet offered.

The round-faced teenager stared at her as if she had just dropped in form another planet. "Talk? About what?"

"Well…my name is Violet Sheldon. I'm from this side of Bronte. My house is just down that lane where I got on the bus. About a quarter of a mile…" She hesitated. When there was no response, she continued, "I'm on my way to see my sister in Dallas; it's my birthday tomorrow. And Lydia—Daddy and I just called her Sissy, you know—Sissy always invites me to spend the day with her on my birthday. Sort of a little tradition, you know."

Her words drifted off into silence, but when the silence continued and Violet was certain the girl's life must be ebbing away, she prompted, "…and you are?"

"Oh, 'scuse me. I'm Laurie Fallman. From San Angelo. At

least that's where my dad lives now. I live there too, with him. My mom lives in Fort Worth. I'm going up there to see her. I guess it's kind of a coincidence. It's my mom's birthday tomorrow, too." Laurie indicated a designer shopping bag wedged between the side of the bus and her feet. "I didn't get her much. Not that it's any big deal or anything..."

Laurie's voice trailed off as she turned to stare at the receding landscape. Baked brown hills covered with wiry, tenacious honey mesquite and interspersed with prickly pear, yucca and dusty clumps of broom grass monopolized the view. Occasionally, behind the ever-present barriers of cattle fence and barbed wire could be seen deer grazing with the lean Brahmas or fat Herefords Texas cattlemen doted on.

"God, there's nothin' out here. What's it like livin' so far from anything? I'd be bored outta my skull!" Laurie emphasized the last three words but never looked at Violet's face for her reply.

"Oh, it's not so bad as you might think, my dear."

"But there aren't even any boys out here," she whined.

"Maybe not so many now, but things were a little different here when I was a girl your age," Violet said. "We're almost to Abilene. Lots of cowboys in Abilene when I was a girl. Over in Sweetwater, too.

"Yeah?" Laurie was listening now, intently studying Violet's face for the first time.

Oh, the wrinkles, Violet thought. She restrained the hand that threatened to call attention to the lines and valleys that marked her years. That's all anyone ever sees anymore. If only this shallow little girl could have seen me when I was young. When I was the most beautiful girl this side of Dallas! And everyone knew it!

"My daddy named me for my violet eyes, you know."

"Really?" The girl looked closer, peering into Violet's eyes. "Hey, they really are violet, aren't they!"

Violet, ignoring the girl—she surmised that Laurie was probably not very bright, and probably totally self-absorbed anyway—continued her soliloquy.

"I was the apple of my daddy's eyes. He was rich too, you know!"

"Really?"

Violet paused again, lifted her chin, and looked through her bifocals at this monosyllabic adolescent. "Yes, my dear, really." She was hoping her abruptness would serve to curb Laurie's interruptions.

"He liked me much better than Sissy, or even Mamma for that matter! He was a wealthy man...owned acres and acres of land. Why, we had the largest ranch in Bronte, back then. Of course, when the war started, he had to leave. Well, when he was killed 'somewhere in the Pacific,' you know, well—I did believe my heart was going to bust wide open, and everything inside me would spill out on the ground!"

Her slight fist tapped her chest and then she flung her arms wide. Tears welled in her eyes as she spoke, and hard little lines tightened downward at the corners of her mouth. Almost immediately, however, she recovered with a sigh and a smile.

"When I was nineteen, Daddy bought a brand-new Packard automobile. It was the most beautiful automobile I'd ever seen. All black and shiny. Hum," she laughed. "Why, I can still see my reflection in that car!" She rested her head on the back of the seat and closed her eyes to drink in the memory. "Those seats were the finest, plushest velour, too. Not this old vinyl stuff they started usin' after the war!" Violet grimaced and slapped the seat covering in disdain.

"Did he let you drive the car much?"

Violet remembered the girl and shot her a withering look.

"Why, of course! Curtis Mahan lived down the road a few miles from us. Down in Tennyson, maybe you remember passin' it before my stop?"

Laurie shook her head and returned a blank stare and half smile.

"Anyway," Violet waved her off, "as soon's my Daddy brought that car home, I grabbed Sissy, who really was a sissy, you know, couldn't even drive a stick shift automobile, even though she was a year older than me, and we drove straight down to see Curtis.

"His daddy owned a very large ranch in Tennyson. The biggest spread there. Over 3,000 acres. Not quite as large as my Daddy's though, you know. Well, Curtis Mahan was without a doubt the handsomest boy outside of Abilene and, mind you, there were some handsome fellas in Abilene. He was tall, dark as an Indian — and Oh! He was strong. I was so in love with Curtis," she sighed. "Everyone said that we were the perfect couple. We were going to get married that very summer. I thought then that I was the luckiest girl in the whole wide world. I had my Daddy, and I would soon be Mrs. Curtis Mahan!"

Ecstasy of past memories lit her face and then suddenly vanished. After a moment, she continued, "I didn't know it then, the day Sissy and I first drove that Packard down to see Curtis, but I found out later—Sissy was in love with Curtis, too. She turned his head. That little tramp..." Violet's jaw tightened, her face became hard, her eyes narrowed, full of hatred. Her fists clenched until the thin, translucent skin of her knuckles seemed to disappear across the white bone beneath. Then, suddenly, she seemed to remember where she was, and that time had far removed her from the day she discovered the treachery of the man she loved and her own sister.

"Look, we're in Abilene, the bus is pulling in." Laurie, appearing grateful for the opportunity, interrupted Violet. "I have to use the john. You better go too, Mrs. Sheldon; it's gonna be a long ride from here to Fort Worth."

"It's Miss Sheldon, my dear. I never married."

"Oh...well. You might need a Coke or something."

Violet emerged into the late evening glow of the once bustling cattle town. The vermillion orb of the setting sun bathed the streets and buildings in its peculiar light. The intensity of the summer heat softened with the setting sun and the bent, stoop-shouldered little woman pulled on her sweater.

The bus driver called a ten-minute stop. As Laurie ran first for new batteries and then for the lady's room, Violet dug for a few quarters and deposited them in the Coke machine. It rattled and clanked, then delivered the dewy red and silver can with a vengeance. Never having trusted these things, she was certain that by the time the can had made its furious descent, the liquid was so shaken and jostled that its contents would explode. She held the can at arm's length before she snapped the top open.

Violet stood in the fading light, sipping delicately, as a soft breeze ruffled the hem of her chiffon. The breeze carried with it the soft scent of sage and dry desert. Her eyes looked beyond the station, beyond the town, out across the barrens of the surrounding hills. These were the same hills she and Curtis had roamed wild and free that summer before the war. The wind rose and she could almost hear Curtis' voice carrying on it.

Laurie returned presently, batteries in hand, examining the zipper fly of her jeans.

"That's where it happened, you know." Violet indicated with a nod toward the east. To Laurie's puzzled look, she continued, "Up on that ridge. That's where they found Curtis' body. It was after the war...still in '45. Curtis finished serving his country. He didn't seem to be scared by the fighting like some of the other boys around here. It's ironic, isn't it? To come through an entire world war without so much as a scratch—They said his horse must have been spooked by a rattlesnake or badger or something. Plenty of both up there."

The old woman and young girl stood silently together, gazing back across time, one caught in her past, the other not yet old enough or wise enough to understand that each heartbeat gone by was her past.

"Time to go, ladies," the driver called.

Laurie spent the next few hours plugged in to her life support system. Violet dozed.

"Looks like we're almost to Fort Worth," Laurie remarked.

Outside their window, the night scenery had changed from occasional sights emanating from the low, squat ranch houses to spotlights on the facades of towering, overdone mansions sporting Greco-Roman columns and ghostly floor-to-ceiling windows. Soon the east-bound highway lanes increased from two to three, then four, and restless buildings began to crowd in upon one another in a hodgepodge of old and new, large and small, business and domicile.

"I'm sure your mother will be very happy to see you." Violet spoke softly in the dimness of the bus.

"Yeah, like I said, I didn't get her much. Just a paisley scarf." She indicated the package again. "I hope she likes it. She was a 60s flowerchild, and I thought she might like paisley...sort of for remembering when she was my age, you know. So maybe she's gonna like it."

"I'm certain she will like it very much," Violet said.

"I was thinking, while you were asleep and all, about what you told me. That's really sad. I mean, about losing your dad and then Curtis like that," Laurie said.

Violet bent her head and smoothed her dress.

"You said you didn't know that Sissy and Curtis were in love that day, the day you drove the car over, that day before the war. When did you find out?"

Violet's gaze focused again on nothing in particular, but turned inward, to the past.

"I didn't find out for certain until after the war. It was the day he came home." Her voice could not hide the bitterness she felt. "Oh! How I remember that day! By the time Curtis was discharged, Daddy had been dead for almost a year," she continued.

"What with him gone, and Mamma not a very good manager and everything, we were already starting to sell off our grazing land. I was near total despair. Mamma's heart was broken. She was almost as devastated as I was, but I still had Curtis, you see. And when Curtis got off that train in Abilene, I fairly flew into his arms. I could feel his arms around me, but Sissy had come with me to meet him, too, and even in Curtis's arms again after what seemed to be an eternity apart...well, I was such a sensitive girl —I felt — I knew, that something was not right. Something had changed. Maybe it was that he just didn't hold me as tight as before...something...I knew! I pushed him off so I could see his face, and it was as plain as it could be. He wasn't even looking back at me! There was nothing for me — nothin' but pure longing in his eyes for her! He was looking right past me at Sissy! They were actually holding each other with their eyes ...

"'Curtis! My darling! No!' I looked from one of them to the other, and I can remember shoutin' and blubberin' like a little baby. I could hear the questioning and the fear in my own voice. I can still hear it. I wanted to shake him to pieces; I know I tried. My whole world had just ripped apart! I was literally pleading for him to pay attention to me, but it was no use. They were infatuated with each other — 'irreversibly drawn together' as you might say. Sissy tried her best to explain it to me later, to say how so very sorry she was … she said that 'they couldn't deny their true love for each other anymore.' What could I do … ?"

She looked down at the shadows of the large blue veins running like highway routes across the maps that were her hands. Why do they look so much more ancient at night, she wondered and sighed.

The driver maneuvered the bus expertly into the Fort Worth terminal, and the doors swung open.

Laurie searched the platform. "There's my mom! I've got to get my bag. Come with me to meet her."

The three stood on the platform of the bus terminal exchanging pleasantries until the driver called for Violet to board the bus. She had spoken kindly and glowingly to Laurie's mother in praise of the girl's company. She was polite enough not to mention her thoughts that the Teen was rather shallow and might benefit from a trial separation from her Walkman.

In the absence of Laurie, Violet moved to the window seat. The bus rolled steadily through the empty streets. As she was settling into the rhythm of flashing streetlights and the glare of headlights from passing cars, something brushed her leg. It was Laurie's package — her birthday present for her mother. She slipped the gold foil-wrapped gift from its designer shopping bag. The flawlessly wrapped box was tied together with an ivory ribbon looped in the center into a perfect bow. Obviously, Laurie had had the gift shop-wrapped. The job was too perfect for something the girl would have done herself.

"Well, it will do no good to try to find your owner," she said as she ran her fingers over the perfect package. "I wouldn't have a clue where to start to find Laurie."

Violet held the package on her lap and stared out into the passing night. She dozed.

"We're here, Ma'am." She felt the driver's hand gently touch her shoulder.

"Oh! Yes. We are in Dallas, aren't we?"

She collected her things, her sweater, purse, blue flower-covered valise, and the designer shopping bag containing the perfectly wrapped paisley scarf, then stepped into the damp coolness of the Dallas night.

Violet left the terminal and walked the block-and-a-half to the Ardmore Hotel. There she roused the disgruntled desk clerk and registered for two nights. The dim, shabby elevator lifted her and all her belongings to the second floor and Room 210.

The room was stale and stuffy and smelled slightly of cigarettes and old wine, but Violet had become accustomed to it over the years.

She sat on the edge of the broken-down mattress with its stained bedspread rumpled beneath her and rested a moment.

"I need a bath," she mumbled. Wearily and with an effort, she forced herself into the bathroom.

After she had adjusted the water to a steamy temperature, she returned to the bed and removed her lavender chiffon. She left her slip on as she laid the dress across the foot of the bed. Suddenly, her attention was again drawn to the designer shopping bag. She removed Laurie's mother's birthday present and lay it in the center of the dingy mattress. It looked so out of place — almost glowing in the shadowy room. Violet stood staring at the package for a few moments, then padded on stockinged feet into the bathroom and turned the water off.

She returned to sit on the edge of the bed and placed the present on her lap.

"I am so tired of being alone," she whispered and then, as if speaking to Laurie, she said:

"You know, Sissy doesn't really live in Dallas. Actually, I don't know where Sissy lives. Hum, I don't even know if she's still alive. I think she is...I believe I would have felt it somehow...if she had died.

"Every year on my birthday, I come back here, to this same shoddy, dump of a hotel. You'd think they'd remember me here, but they don't.

"Why do I come here?" Her fingers played across the satiny softness of the ribbon as she looked to her side, as if she were again seated beside Laurie.

"Because...I suppose I have to keep up appearances...the neighbors, you know."

"You see, after Daddy was killed in the war, and after Curtis died up there on the ridge and Mamma died of her broken heart and Sissy ran off and vowed never to lay eyes on me again...well, I lost all the land. Everything except the house and garden. I was totally despondent, you see.

"Everyone blamed me for killing Curtis, and...and I suppose I did..." Frown lines creased her brow, and the corners of her mouth turned downward as she stared at the ancient carpet.

As if puzzled now, she continued, "You know, I remember wanting him dead. I remember that hunting trip up on the ridge. Sissy and Curtis were riding along the ridge together, and I...I stepped out on the rail in front of them. I slipped when I fired my rifle...I must have jumped out on some loose shale...everything was so fast. I was going to kill them both, you see. Curtis and Sissy. But the rifle fired into the air, and Curtis's horse reared and he fell backwards, and his head smashed open and his brains poured out on the rocks. Sissy's horse spooked and wheeled and ran back down the trail toward our campsite. I just stood there, holding my rifle and watching her on her horse and Curtis's horse running off down the trail. Mr. Mahan, Curtis's dad, pulled her off her horse when they stampeded into camp. He said she was in hysterics, and all he could understand was her screaming that Curtis was dead.

"He died instantly. I dropped my rifle and ran to him as soon as Sissy was gone. I can still see him lying there, just staring up at the sky. I kissed him goodbye and closed his eyes, you know. He belonged to me, after all.

"Sissy never told anyone what I had done, I suppose. She just left one day and never came back. I think Mr. Mahan guessed. He never spoke to me again and never looked at me again, either. People around town started pointing, and sometimes I heard them all whispering behind my back, but I didn't pay them any mind at all, you know.

"I got lonesome, though, after they were all gone, so I started coming here, to Dallas, every year on my birthday. Used to, I'd just come here and find some company for a few days, you know...a gentleman friend. Now I just come here. People back home think I come up to Dallas because Sissy invites me for my birthday every year."

With the faint sound of dripping water in the bath, she bowed her head, paused, and wiped a stray tear from her cheek, then carefully untied the ivory ribbon from the gold box. Gently she lifted the paisley scarf from the folds of tissue paper surrounding it.

"Why! It's got violet in it, and shades of lavender, too!" she exclaimed, holding the shimmering scarf out in the dim light. Then she jumped to her feet, laughing merrily as she wrapped the perfect paisley scarf around her thin, bare shoulders. "Sissy, darling! It's exquisite! What a wonderful birthday present! It really is true! You definitely are the most wonderful sister in the whole wide world!"

And in a world filled with streetlights, passing cars, honking horns, and wine-besotted derelicts, Violet Sheldon danced, danced, danced around the dingy room—alone again.

Amelia's Legacy

The sun had long ago reached its apex and was beginning a slow descent behind a line of billowing silver-tipped clouds. There it produced a fiery mix of evening orange and deep purple that mellowed to grey where it blended into the far line of the oceanic horizon. Possibly it was the changing light that finally woke her. She did not move immediately, however. Not only was she exhausted, sore and disheveled, but she thought she was probably suffering from a bad case of sunburn as well.

She lay still for several minutes until she could no longer tolerate her awkward position. Slowly, in spite of the pain, she sat up. Pulling her leather jacket from the sand near her feet, she used it as a cushion to rest her sore back on the trunk of a palm. Though extremely weary and still a little dazed, she began to assess her situation. Looking behind her, she took in the island upon whose shores she rested. From what she could see, which wasn't a great deal, it consisted of a dense tangle of vines, coconut palms, and mangos, all of which starkly contrasted with the shimmering blueness that encircled it.

Georgiana was still reeling from the crash. For someone usually as verbal as herself, "endless" was the only word she could come up with to describe her Pacific view. "Lush" was the only word she could use to describe the jungle behind her. Ironically, that was also the only word she could come up with to describe the man who was responsible for her being here, utterly alone, for all she knew. Matthew Youngblood. What if he really was killed in the crash? The plane went down, where? Out there, in the gentle surf? It was so beautiful. What right had they to crash headlong into such beauty? She wrapped her arms across her chests the temperature had begun to drop fast with the setting sun, and her teeth began to chatter. She put the jacket on and would have left the beach, the jungle might be warmer, but she needed time to think and, out here, things might be a little clearer, less tangled.

Matt had enticed her on this journey, this odyssey, this catastrophe, she thought, her anger rising. Why had she let him talk her into this?

She let her mind wander back to a few days ago. She had been comfortable, resting in the hotel on Papua after the long shoot. It seemed the older she got, the quicker she tired of the 12 and 14-hour days on location, and she had decided to stay over for an extra weekend after the rest of the crew had flown back to L.A. She had not realized that Matt Youngblood, a freelance photographer, had been staying in the same hotel until she ran into him in the Melbourne Room bar.

"Georgiana Hyatt ...!"

She lifted her eyes in the dim, smoke-filled room and saw him making his way through the packed bar toward her. She did not know how she had missed seeing him the moment she walked in. Matt was, as always, breathtakingly handsome. Tall, rakish, yet with boyish charm, he had an adventurer's look about him. He wore his brown fedora "Indiana Jones" style, although he was a little taller and darker than the movie hero. Each time she saw him again, and the absences usually spanned several years, she wondered anew why they had never slept together. He was as close to an Adonis as anyone she had ever seen. Maybe that was it. Maybe he was a little too perfect, too magnificent.

"...Georgie!" He swept her into his arms as they came together, their lips met and she felt the fire of his intense passion as he kissed her long and hard. Suddenly, time and place no longer mattered, and any resistance she may had felt left her. She submitted to his will. Matt was the center of the universe, all she had ever longed for. Then, suddenly, he released his iron grip on her limp body, the moment passing. Awkwardly she returned to reality.

"Where's the hubby?" he said, still holding her, smiling mischievously.

"Ah...Matt...it is so good to see you again. I'm not married," she mumbled, still locked in his spell. She wondered, idiotically, if she should perhaps shake his hand now. Instead she stood, catching her breath, studying those boyish features, drowning in his deep, dark eyes.

"In that case, may I join you?" he already held a Scotch whiskey in his hand. She hadn't noticed it when he crossed the room. Before she could reply, he pulled out her chair and another for himself.

"What'er you doing on Papua, Georgie?" He listened intently as she told him of the new line of South Pacific swimwear Intaglio Design was promoting, and how she was now their top model. He downed his Scotch, ordered another for himself and a vodka Collins for her. By the time the waiter brought their drinks, he had explained that he had just finished a World Environs assignment on New Guinea and just flown over to Papua for some change of scenery.

"I discovered this great old twin-engine Lockheed Electra. Bought it on the spot. Completely restored. I've been flying myself all over the islands, paying my way by shipping off photos at each stop. It's been terrific, Georgie. I wish you could take some more time off and come with me. I'm flying off to the Marshal's tomorrow. I need to stop on Guam..."

Similar backgrounds and mutual acquaintances allowed the conversation to flow easily between the supermodel, just passing her prime, and the world-class photographer. The two sat together long into the evening, sipping their drinks, talking of the people they knew and the places they had been, the near misses, and the times they had connected. Later, walking the beach barefoot, both speaking of other things, but telling of the thousand reasons they were each still alone, he held her again, and he whispered again, softly, so enticing, "... come with me Georgie."

That night, perhaps because of the magic of the South Pacific, perhaps because of their long unrequited desire, they did not remain apart. Their lovemaking was as Georgie had always imagined, made so much more by passionate by the longing, the sea air, and the faraway island that held them close.

In the morning, Matt took her to see the Electra. It was beautiful, sleek and shining, a silver aluminum masterpiece. It belonged in the sky, she thought.

"Come and fly with me, Georgie. It'll great up there together, you'll see! Fly with me." Matt would not be denied.

"It's so old ... is it safe to fly?"

"Perfectly. It's been completely and meticulously restored," he said, patting the fuselage. "I updated the radio and added a few bells and whistles, of course. But this beauty will take us anywhere we want to go in these islands."

Standing back, Georgie frowned, her hands shoved deep in the pockets of her leather jacket. "Something ... something seems so familiar about this plane," she said.

"Maybe you remember seeing photos of one just like it. It's the same model Earhart and Noonan were flying when they disappeared out here."

"Oh, God!"

"Hold on, Georgie! It's not the same plane. It's one like it. Anyway, they probably went down because of navigational problems, off course, out of gas, you know. There weren't any malfunctions of the aircraft."

"How do you know?" she demanded.

"Relax, Georgie. This baby's sound as a 747," he said reassuringly. Then her folded her in his powerful arms and kissed her long and deep, and she forgot everything else, even her apprehensions.

"Okay, so where're we going?" she asked as she fastened her seat belt.

"Well, we're headed for Howland. I've got to get some natural-habitat photos..."

"Did you say Howland?" Georgie screamed above the roar of the engine as the aircraft lifted into flight.

"Yeah! There's a small strip there. Marine biologists use it all the time. Won't be any problem landing there."

"Isn't that the same damn field Earhart landed on just before she vanished?!" This was all a little beyond coincidental; Georgie began to worry.

"You're not superstitious, are you Georgie?"

Sitting here now, darkness closing in around her, she damn well wished she had been superstitious. She wished she had demanded that Matt turn the plane around that very instant and take her back. But that was yesterday.

A full moon hung directly above now, playing its flickering yellow-white light across the waves in a phantom, iridescent glow. A canopy of stars, hanging just above her head, adorned the indigo sky. Waves washed onto the beach in a steady, low roar, moving ever closer with the rising tide. They licked at the sand near her feet, hissed softly, then receded into the smooth, wet sand. Georgie huddled beneath the palm, wrapped against the night breeze, lonelier than she had ever been in her life.

She needed water and food. Tomorrow could not come soon enough.

Thirst and hunger gnawed at her. The mindless bliss of sleep eluded her. The sandwiches and thermos of strong coffee they had shared to clear their heads from the liquor of the previous night had long since disappeared...drinks together a few nights ago...an age ago, she thought. The rest of the food on board certainly went down with the Electra. Her head dropped to her hands, her elbows on her bent knees.

She couldn't remember much about the actual plane crash, she realized. Did they land in the ocean or on this island? She couldn't see any debris around her. She did remember that they somehow got off course and were running low on fuel. Of course, the radio had gone out and the radar wasn't working right either. It was like something straight out of a very bad movie. She laughed out loud at the irony of it all, while steady streams of silent tears coursed the smudges on her face.

Suddenly she remembered watching in horror as Matt fought for control of the airplane. Her last words came back to her now. "We're dead, aren't we, Matt!" She couldn't remember his reply or even if he did reply. Overwhelmed, Georgie abandoned herself to her tears and the lonely, starry night.

Finally, she slept, although fitfully tossing from side to side. She was never able to find a comfortable position, and she was not used to the incessant roar of the ocean. By morning, she was famished, and her tongue was swollen from thirst. She was cramped so badly that she was not certain she would be able to walk, but she knew she had to try; she had to pee. Every movement seemed a monumental effort, hardly worth it. First her swollen tongue, then her stiff neck, arms, back, and finally, she stretched her cramped legs, groaning with every new effort. All systems go! If nothing else worked, she would bully her body into compliance. With all the strength she could muster, she pushed to her feet and walked into the dense underbrush to relieve herself. Modesty first.

"I don't know why I'm being so damned modest," she said aloud, astonished at the loudness of her own voice.

"Well, you damned well ought to be in a tropical paradise like this; you never know who the hell's going to be combing these beaches," a masculine voice replied to her own.

Georgie's heart skipped several beats. When she came out of the cover of the vines, her heart was still pounding crazily from her sudden fright.

She struggled with the thought of killing him on the spot — if she wasn't certain she wasn't already dead, she might consider it — an instantaneous thought. Instead, she rushed into his arms in gratitude for being alive, here with her. She wasn't alone after all.

"Matthew" My God, what happened to you? Where in hell were you? I looked all up and down this beach for you yesterday. I didn't see a trace...."

He drew her reluctant body to him and held her close to his chest. "When the plane hit the water, it flipped. You must have been thrown clear almost instantly. I stayed with it as long as I could ... got out as much gear as I could. I got a few supplies before she went down, flashlight, batteries, some of our food and some drinking water, not much really. The tide carried you in before I could get to you. The plane rested on the edge of the reef for a while, and I had to keep diving as long as I could. When the tide changed. It pulled the plane off the ledge, and it went down into deep water."

"Did you get a chance..."

"No," he said softly. "the plane was too old. It didn't have a transponder. There was no way to send an emergency signal. Com'on, come with me. I hauled everything around to the north side of the island. I got a chance to spot a little lagoon surrounded by some cliffs. We can probably find some shelter there, and you need some water and something to eat. I've already laid in a supply of really fresh coconuts this morning," he said with his old characteristic smile.

Georgie looked into his sunburned face, already polished to a shine by the Pacific wind. A stubble of beard adorned his angular jaw.

"This isn't a joke, Matt. It's not a game or some...some wild adventure photo shoot of yours! We are lost out here, and no one knows where we are!"

"Com'on Georgie! It doesn't help a damned thing for you to get hysterical over this! We're here now and, by God, we're gonna make the best of it! Now com'on." He grabbed her arm and pulled. She winced, jerked her arm free, glared at him, and then followed stiffly when he turned his back and walked off. She looked back up her beach one last time. Perhaps she might need to come back — retrace her steps for some reason — but the tide had already washed their tracks away.

He led her in a shortcut through the scraggly palms that adorned the eastern tip of the island. Presently, they emerged on the northern shore. It was as if they had entered a completely different world. The beach she had just left had been clean and white, but what little beach she could see here was littered with sharp lava, volcanic rock, and odd flotsam.

"I've just about got everything over here already," he said, satisfied with his own efforts. He handed her a canteen of water and opened a watertight container that held the last of their sandwiches. "Easy on the water until we can locate some here," he said. "Coconut water can keep us alive, but it'll give ya the runs, too."

She looked at him now with a growing realization of the real gravity of their plight.

"If worse comes to worse," he held up a fistful of crumpled plastic wrap, "I can rig a little contraption to catch condensation."

She knew he was doing his best to reassure her.

"Why did you wait so long to find me. You should have come looking for me right away, Matt," she said, accusation rising in her voice. She was mad at herself the instant she said it. She needed Matt on her side more than ever now. It served little purpose to make him an enemy now. Still, she was finding it hard not to blame him for their situation.

"I did," he said, unruffled by her accusing tone. "I found you last night. You were asleep. I didn't want to wake you, so I just kept working till daylight. I kept an eye on you. You're not saying you wanted to help me move everything last night, are you?"

"No..."

"Com'on. See that lagoon over there?" He pointed to a small horseshoe curve in the shoreline about a quarter of a mile away. "I waited for you to check it out."

She followed him along the rocky shoreline and onto the little beach that surrounded the calm, crystal clear lagoon on three sides. The white sand stretched from the water's edge about thirty yards back up the island where it suddenly rose sharply into a rocky cliff. He led her away from the water's edge, back along the rock-strewn base of the cliff. The going was tricky and she was becoming tired, her thoughts wandering to what she would be doing today if she were back in L.A., working as usual, when suddenly, they were back on the sandy floor of a beach facing a hollow in the cliff's wall.

"A cave!"

"You wait here..."

"Not on your life," she said. "I'm not going to stay here while you wander in there and get lost forever!"

He studied her face for a moment, "You're right. That was foolish. We should stick together now. Let's go back and get the flashlight and the rope."

He was headed back up the beach before she could protest.

"Alright, we're tied off," he said as he finished wedging the piece of driftwood between two rocks at the cave's entrance. He tested it with a couple of full-body tugs, nodded to himself and stepped into the dark, gaping hole. Georgie followed; actually, she had little choice as they were tied together, "Just in case," Matt had said.

"Do you think there are bats in here?"

"No. There are no bats on these islands. You're safe, Georgie," he said. "You're only imagining bats because it's a cave.

Georgie swallowed her rising fear. She had always been slightly claustrophobic, and her imagined bats certainly were not going to help this situation. She would still rather be with Matt, though, than outside, waiting and wondering, she rationalized.

They followed the opening about twenty more feet before the light beam revealed a narrow passage, turning sharply to the left. "Let's go," Matt said. So far, they had crouched through the cave, but as soon as they stepped through the passageway, they found themselves in a large, high-ceilinged chamber, they could stand upright now. Remarkably, the chamber was not completely black. Light filtered through a slice in the rocks on the sloping wall to their right, and in the stillness, they could hear the steady, echoing drip of water from a seep in the rocks onto the chamber floor.

Matt quickly located the water source beneath the chamber's window. The water tasted slightly of minerals, but it was fresh. He set his canteen beneath the drip to collect the precious liquid.

"This solves our drinking-water problem," he said.

Georgie rested beside the seep as Matt, freed from his tether, began to explore. She closed her eyes in the dim light, moved her hand back to brace her still-sore back and gave a startled cry. Matt rushed back toward her.

"What is it?"

"Something ... there!" She pointed down.

He played the light on the ground surrounding them. There, just to the right of the seep, lay an old leather flight jacket, similar to the ones they now wore, only much, much older. Matt was reaching for the jacket when his light caught something else. About ten feet away were the remnants of an old fire pit, barely discernable in the layer of dust and debris that covered it.

"Someone's been living here, Georgie," he said.

He played the light beam around the perimeter of the little nook of the chamber at the water seep.

"Look!"

Both of them cautiously walked closer to the chalky gray mass.

"My God. It's a human skeleton," Georgie said in horror.

"Must be the owner of this jacket. By the looks of what's left, whoever it was, was broken up pretty badly. Look," Matt said, "the ribcage is busted all to pieces. The left leg is fractured, and the right arm is broken up pretty good, too."

Matt stepped closer for a better look and kicked something loose with his foot.

"What is that?"

"Well," he retrieved a round leather tube from beneath his foot. "It looks like some kind of document carrier. He took the handkerchief from his back pocket and wiped off a layer of dust.

"Here, hold the flashlight. Look, there are some initials embossed on it, an F and, I believe that's an N." He paused thoughtfully before repeating the initials. "F.N."

"You don't suppose..." Georgie said.

"Suppose what?"

"That that's Fred Noonan's case...that that's Fred Noonan!" She pointed to the skeletal remains that leaned on the side of the chamber.

"What...no! You're letting your imagination run wild now," Matt said, yet there was a hint of uncertainty in his rebuke.

"What's in there?"

He opened the case. "Nothing, it's empty."

"Damn!"

"What did you think? You'd solved the puzzle of Amelia Earhart?" He laughed. "You're being sort of romantic, aren't you?"

"Maybe. It would be exciting, though, wouldn't it? To finally solve the mystery. Besides, there's nothing that says that isn't the body of Fred Noonan, is there? After all, isn't this real close to where they were last heard from?"

"Well, I guess..." He shrugged his broad shoulders and grinned his boyish grin.

Suddenly he stopped short, frozen in place.

"What!?" Her eyes followed his to the gapping fissure, the window in the chamber wall. There was nothing.

"Nothing!" He appeared shaken, but regrouped quickly, drawing her attention back to himself. "Nothing ... You were saying...?"

She eyed him suspiciously but continued, "I was saying that those are Fred Noonan's remains, and Amelia Earhart's remains must be somewhere close by, right on this very island!" She spoke almost triumphantly.

"Well let's just go get our shovels and get busy and we can probably dig 'em up real quick-like!" Matt was sarcastically mocking her now. His impatience was evident with his rising voice. The two faced off in the dim light.

"Let's get out of here." Matt broke the ice that had suddenly developed between them. "We shouldn't use up all the juice in these flashlight batteries."

As soon as they emerged into the strong light and fresh air of the lagoon, Georgie stopped him.

"What is wrong with you? Just because I think those are Fred Noonan's remains, you're angry with me? What gives here, Matt?"

"Not a damned thing gives here, Georgie!" He tore himself from her grasp and headed off down the beach toward their meager salvaged possessions.

He was becoming extremely short with her now, and she didn't like it...not one bit. She ran after him.

"Look, Matt! Just because I'm a romantic, and it would be sort of neat to maybe be the ones to solve a real mystery that's over fifty years old..."

"Alright! You solved it! Okay!?"

His words sent her reeling. "What?" she said to his once-again retreating form. And once again, she had to run to stop him.

"Where are you going in such a hurry. What do you mean, 'I solved it?' Stop!"

"No. I've got to check on our stuff, now."

"Why the rush. We're alone here, aren't we?" She held him now by his jacket lapels. "What did you mean when you said I solved the mystery of Amelia Earhart? What's going..."

She felt his body suddenly tense as he gasped, holding his breath. She turned and followed his gaze, transfixed on something behind her at the top of the cliff.

There, silhouetted along the top of the rocky ledge, stood a frightfully thin figure, leaning on a long staff. Although bent and aged, it was obvious, even from this distance, that the old woman had once been tall, lithe, even aristocratic. As Georgie stared in awe, the woman's wispy short grey hair feathered in the trade winds from the sea.

"A...Amelia..." Georgie suddenly lunged in the direction of the lone figure. Matt grabbed her and held her.

"It's her. I saw her looking at us through the rock crevice in the cavern. It is her, Georgie. She's old, but it'd be hard to mistake those features."

"Matt! We've found her! We've rescued Amelia Earhart! We've..."

"Stop it, Georgie!" He held her hard and shook her. Tears of joy and confusion streaked her beautiful face. "Stop!" His voice had softened now. "Think about this, Georgie. That's Amelia Earhart up there! She's been stranded on this island for over fifty years, Georgie!"

"What? What are you saying, Matt? We've found..."

"Georgie," he stroked the soft tangle of her long hair, looked deeply into her tear-filled eyes, then drew her to him. He held her close, rocking her gently in his embrace.

"I suppose her final flight — her legend, this island, were her legacy, my darling ... and now it's ours. Fifty years," he whispered, "and no one ever came to her rescue, Georgie...what makes you think anyone is coming to ours?"

THE END

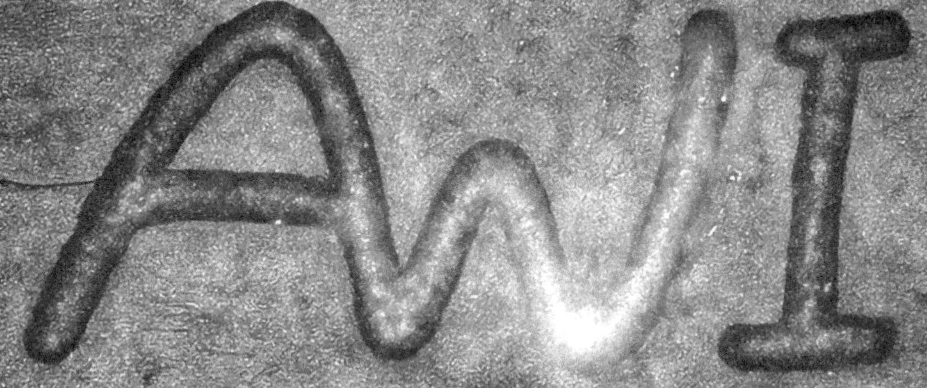

OLD BRANDS

A few poems from 30 years ago ...

The Poetry Trail

by CS Norwood

A SONG FOR 1965

With my lifetime in my pocket,
Eternity in the sole of my shoe.
A will to keep on moving,
Lord, I've found my home.

My home is not for loving.
It moves as does the Westward Wind.
It's been from here to God's heaven,
And it's flowing to the sea.

It's brought me knocking on your garden gate,
I've come to ask you go with me,
If you've a soul for wandering.
Don't ponder long, I'm leaving with the Easterlies.

Ah! But it's a sad soul says farewell,
But you've built your castle here,
And you're bound to live from eight to six,
When I've offered you this wayfaring tide.

Oh, it's commonplace and so very lonely.
Don't think I've shed but one tear,
Freedom will my deathbed be.
If my heart could but stay with thee.
If my heart could but stay with thee ...

Wild where the sea oats grow,
Long past the break of day
I wander on the crystal sand and by the seaswept coast.
Waves joust ships anchored just offshore
while rigging sings along the wind.
I do not know, nor can I tell
the tale of where this song comes from.
But it's caught me here, and I will ever be
Wild where the sea oats grow.

Wild where the sea oats play,
long past the break of day,
there
beats my heart away.

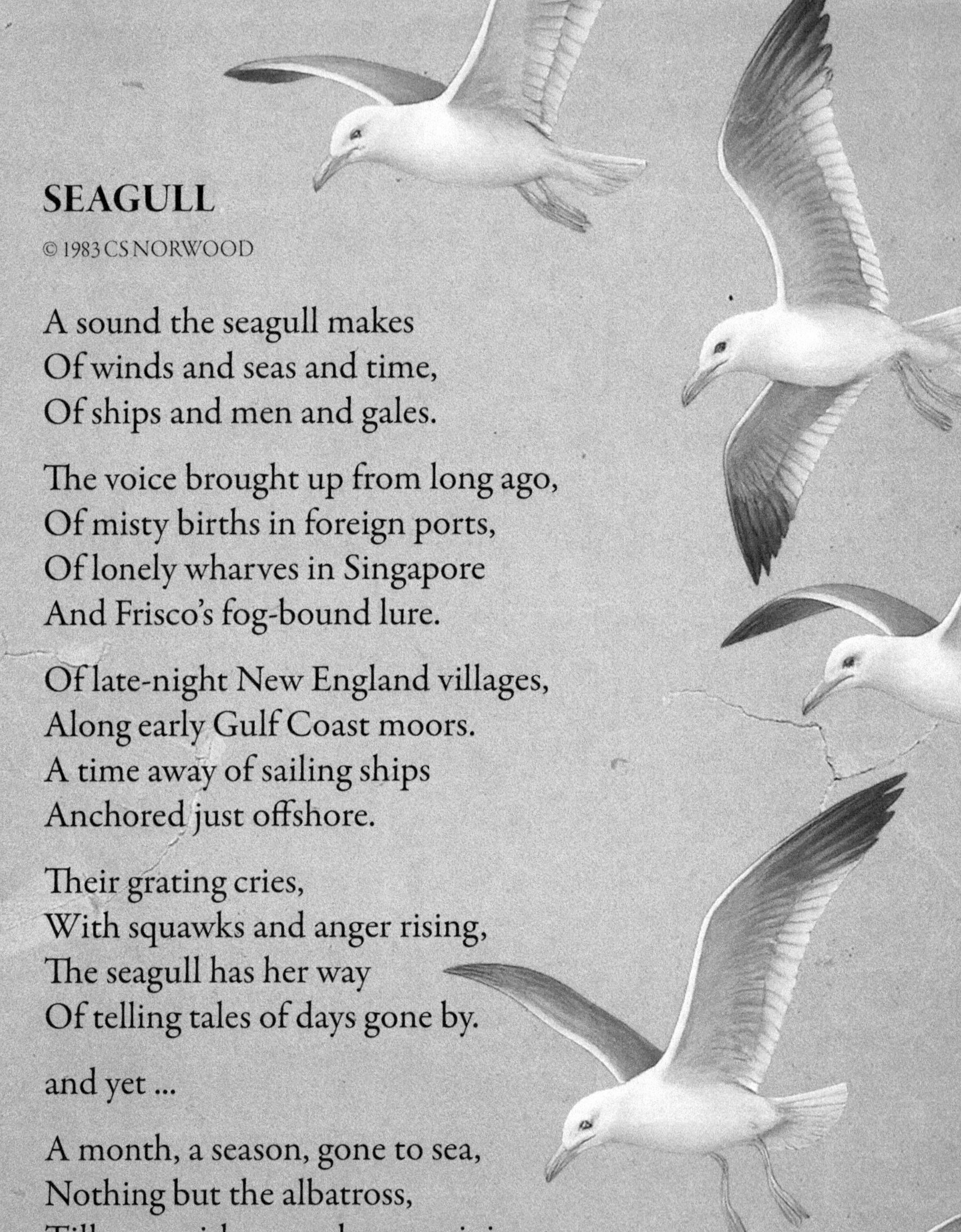

SEAGULL

A sound the seagull makes
Of winds and seas and time,
Of ships and men and gales.

The voice brought up from long ago,
Of misty births in foreign ports,
Of lonely wharves in Singapore
And Frisco's fog-bound lure.

Of late-night New England villages,
Along early Gulf Coast moors.
A time away of sailing ships
Anchored just offshore.

Their grating cries,
With squawks and anger rising,
The seagull has her way
Of telling tales of days gone by.

and yet ...

A month, a season, gone to sea,
Nothing but the albatross,
Till men with weary hearts rejoice, to see
The seagull winging home.

GOOD CAPTAIN

In search of safe harbor,
Seeking respite for these souls,
I have shunned hopelessness.
I have set my course t'ward purling shores.

Lest gashes be torn through her hull,
I post lookout fore and aft.
Seeing all with eyes that cannot waver,
helmsman without grudge or favor.

"See ye yonder rocky shores,
ne'r have heard man's voice afore!
We'll anchor here to rest ourselves,
make ready for the morrow's quest.

"I'll tell ye tales this night on watch,
Of men and ships, this sailor's lot.
We'll speak and drink and ease our weariness.
Tomorrow's work will leave no rest!"

Good Captain sits with pipe in cheek,
to spin his tales, the seaman's lore.
"Within yer bones, m'lads, do ye hear
the call of souls from this endless deep?

"They be there, for all to hear,
On any night when sleep's not near.
I've come to know m'lads,
what the sea calls down, she'll ne'r return!

"Given life and breath when words be spoke,
these spirits sing and dance a mighty hoax!
They raise their voices along a gale,
till ye feel the life within ye pale.

"I'll tell ye this tale so ye'll know tis true.
A man's but bones and tough sinew.
These spirits be the unholy ones to face,
if ye expect to survive this endless race!

"So square yer shoulders, do yer best.
The sea, she'll hand ye all the rest.
Fire brand m'words within yer breast;
ye dare not flinch when comes the test!

"To berth with ye now, I've warned ye well.
Ye'll see this dawn; I'm here to tell.
This sea, she'll look upon yer bravest deeds
and like as not, she'll save ye for her own."

This vessel plays her music sweet,
With wind and rigging sounding sleep.
The steady clang as wave meets hull
resounds through tops'l, main' and all.

***

"Rise up now! This night is done!
There's sails to man, work's begun!
I cannot tell ye, I will not say,
how each of ye will fare this day."

They run on up; they take their posts.
"Ah m'lads! To speak of ye, I cannot boast!
My ship, my crew...
for these, fair ladies, I bade adieu!"

The rigging sings her forged-iron song,
As wind snaps shrouds;
"T 'won't be long we'll see our fate!
Now weigh that anchor, be quick and strong!"

The jib an mains'ls gather breath,
Our ship slices breakers in its quest,
For port is here ne'r silk nor calm,
she waits with not an open arm.

We'll trespass here, we'll cruise the shore,
We'll find our windless cove and more.
We'll have our peace and end this lonely voyage.
Men so stout! Of greatest courage!

"See there! The shoreline receding,
below those cliffs with lush green seeding.
I'll wager an anchorage we'll soon espy.
We'll send longboats in, alight on land that's dry."

"Capt'n! Rocks to portside!" cries the Watch.
"Our ship! Our ship is lost!"
"—Silence, now good lad, I say,
and man yer post this day!

"Duty now, yer honor bound,
Ye've come to sail this world around.
Keep yer wits and show to me,
These rocks of doom within the sea."

"Ah, yes, m'lad, ye've done quite well!
They're there, hidden in the swell.
We'll be right, if that's the lot.
We've good wind and sail to say our course.

"We'll keep these rocks to starboard,
We'll swing her round.
All hands report on deck!
These rocks ahead are more than just a speck!"

To gash her hull, to send her down.
Our ship! Our pride! Our souls to drown!
—Nay! Cannot be!
I've too long fought, man against the sea!

I'll do 'er now!
I'll save the lot! I've not come 'round the world,
To sink my bones 'neath the sea to rot!

—Good Captain; My Captain—
Whispers the wind through mizzen and spar.
Sung so sweetly, I would rest easy.
—To me, your soul belongs—

"Nay!" shouts I,
I've afore heard yer song!
Tis just the moaning of wind 'n wave!
I'll ne'r hand ye what's in m'power to save!

Ah! Then the mighty flecks of foam...
Rushing! Crashing! Tearing! Rending loose
great planks of hull splintered upon the rock.
The surge of salt sea calling home.

No time for thought of futures lost.
No moment to spare for youth gone by.
A man must surely live, then die.
A fate as easily drawn in lots.

A mournful sigh, the last farewell,
from hearts of men so brave and true.
All silence now, save the mighty roar,
of an ageless sea under an indigo sky.

The blackest of nights
washes with wave over ravaged hull.
Souls gone down, retribution's cost!
And the sea regains her serenity.

***

Another dawn bursts forth, a red prevailing,
as a mighty, sinewy hand caresses
a great wheel worn silken from endless touch.
Fathomless eyes in a timeless, weathered face.

A resolution never bending.
An ode to the sea unending:
—"And this!" Roars Captain, "Ye've yet to learn!
What this almighty sea calls down—she'll ne'r return!"

ON! FANCY

I chanced one day a walk to take
along the footpath by the lake.
Wandering slowly the course I'd set
not to waver lest I forget.

Guided now by path well-trod
I'd only to give my fancy a nod.
She raced and cavorted as if a young colt.
I thought this Fancy acted quite bold.

I saw all the gaming I had done as a youth.
I never did reckon with all that was truth.
I would build great armored castles,
bordered my bed with gold-threaded tassels!

I had run to adventure;
as a youth I'd never known censure.
Now time has come to set straight all accounts.
It was like trying to gather mist by the ounce!

She would go; she would come—
my spirit, my life's on the run!
I'll catch her; I'll tie her!
Here she pranced so near; I'll put her on a tether!

Then she raced toward things I could not foresee,
having never really been put in check by me.
Like the course of an arrow now in midflight,
I would have some measure of comfort—not this fright!

Then standing, searching Yonder, I did begin to shiver.
I had no reason to suspect what Fancy would deliver.
What as yet unseen abominations could she bring
and place on my hand like a bride's new ring?

"What you bring to me, it may not be
what I truly wish for my future, you see?!
So, give me some warning!" I shout at the dust,
but she's gone again after some other fanciful lust.

OLD BRANDS

THE STORIED TRAIL CITATIONS

All images conceived and directed by CS Norwood,
with rendering assistance from Microsoft AI, Copilot Jack.

Thanks for joining us along this storied trail, and for more adventures from AWI Old Brands, including exciting upcoming books, visit us on our website by scanning the QR Code below.

AWI - adventure writers ink & Station WIL

THE SKY BETWEEN US:

And the Voices That Bind Us

Three Sisters ||| Three Voices

Gravity

by SL Malvoso

In 2003, I began writing haiku alongside my poems. Unfortunate circumstances often forced me to stop writing for long periods of time, and even work on my paintings became tedious and complex.

This has been a lifelong interest and remains deeply important to me. There was never a clear destination or goal, only the time spent within the unknown journey ahead. Perhaps it has been a way of magnifying the simple, fleeting moments within the life I was given.

I hope you enjoy reading some of my thoughts.

Love to all,
Lynne

GRAVITY

Haikus, Poetry, and Paint

by

Sylvia Lynne Malvoso

Grass yearns colours' green
The Giver remains unseen.

Falling rain answers

— 8/20/17

Words are never heard
They only form an answer
Nature's silence speaks.

— 8/20/17

Mirages dreaming within
Words reach out to hold.

Sunrise arises untold.

— 8/25/17

Evacuation To Alabama

Journeys still undone
Safer now beneath your sun
Storms passed, rhymes begun.

— 9/12/17 (Sisters reunited)

Return Home

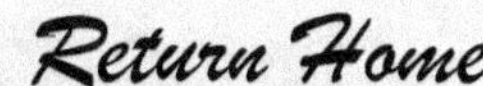

Roof, walls, home concealed
Tiredness rested, sadness healed
Home, safe, hope revealed.

— 9/16/17

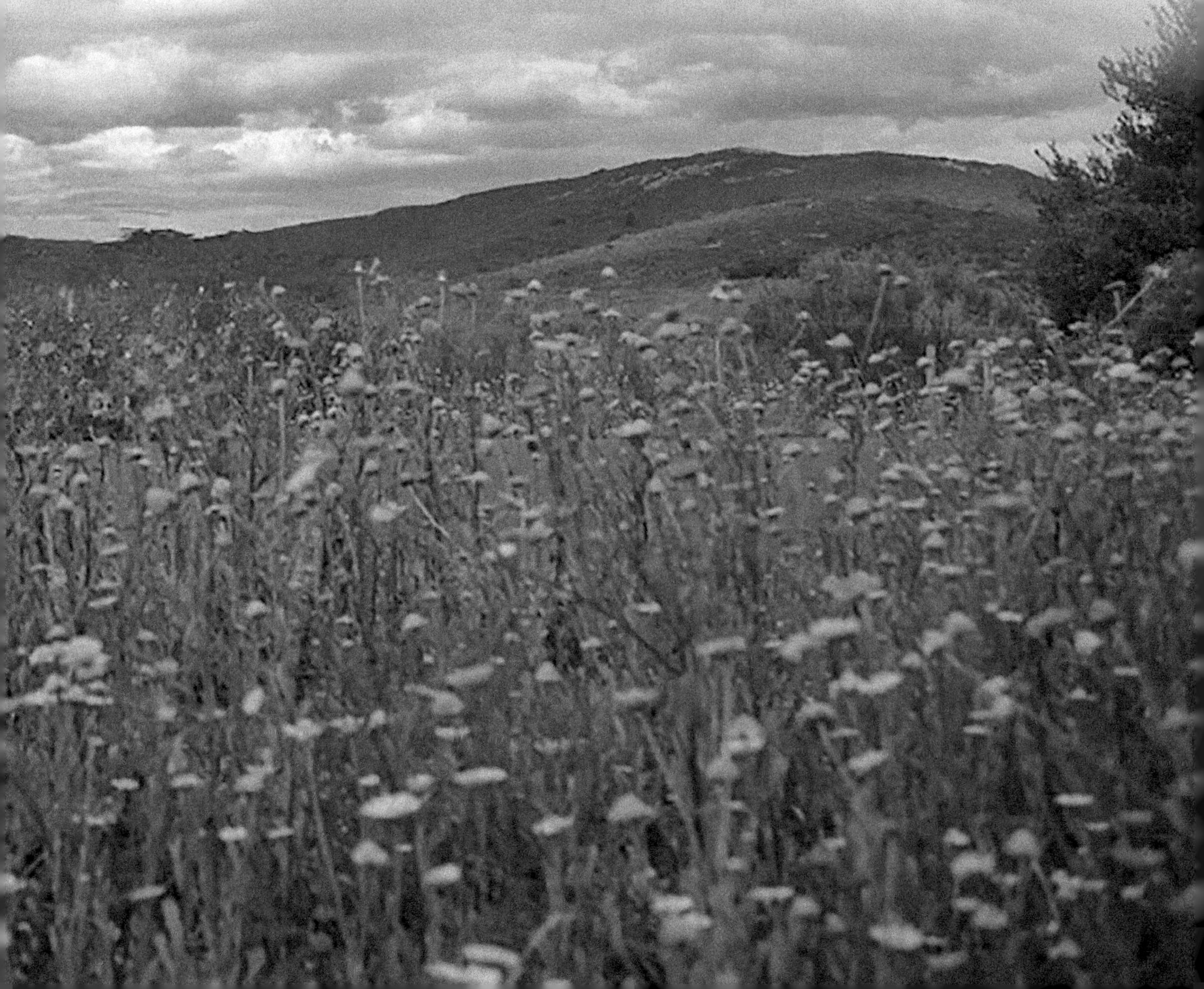

In smallest spaces
Autumn leaves whisper on trees
Of time eternal.

— 10/13/17

Evacuation to Atlanta

Running from our home
Driving towards a fate unknown
All the birds have flown.

— 9/7/17

9/11/17 My rendering of a radar image on from The Weather Channel – Hurricane Irma radar image of the "monsters" that I imaged within the hurricane winds.

Hurricane

Structure's sense decreased
Beastly views of winds unleashed
Destinies unreached.

— 9/11/17

Transformation

Invisible light,
Reflecting nature's unseen,
In thoughts to believe.

Transparent rainbow,
Breaks thru translucent storm clouds.
Hopes form to believe.

Infinite dark skies,
Star light transforms in being,
Knowing to believe.

— 10/16/17

Thoughts seeking answers
Words appear without voices
Words heard through the heart.

— 10/21/17

Shining yellow sun
Stars invisible in blue
Shining light through you.

Awakened

Morning air echoes
Spring's distant roads
where birds sing
Stirring winter's loss.

— 4/20/18

From the Sky

Falling sun gleams high
Draping grace thru salty sky
Tears of water sigh.

— 11/22/17

To offer earth's source
The gift of God's abundance
A hand reaches forth.

— 9/25/18

Some of My Poems

Paintings

Swirling Spheres of Matter

Where did your vanished teardrop go?
On wings to join the clouds that glow,
To feel the light of God's rainbow,
And gather with cool winds that blow?

....

Transformed through love when raindrops flow;
In memories, your greenfields grow.

—2018

Teardrop

Can God be found in endless skies?
Or might I see Him thru your eyes?
Who, what, when, how, where and why,
Does water fall when someone cries?

....

Then Love did speak like silent sighs;
Reflecting light - your teardrop dries.

— 2018

Past 2000

Sky, trees, fields, streams, living scene
Inside outside live.
Black, blue, flat screens, world now seen.

— 4/29/18

Each New Day

Dreams at nighttime did not last
Earth traveled miles till darkness passed
Returning once more to the sun
Ahead the distance just begun.

While whirling spinning throughout space
Earth held me gently in my place
Embraced by all its gravity
I did not move but earth moved me

We have arrived awake to learn
A choice of purpose to discern
The value of the days we spend
Till precious daylight once more ends.

We have arrived in strange new land
In space where no one else can stand
To witness different points of view
Perceived by no one else like You.

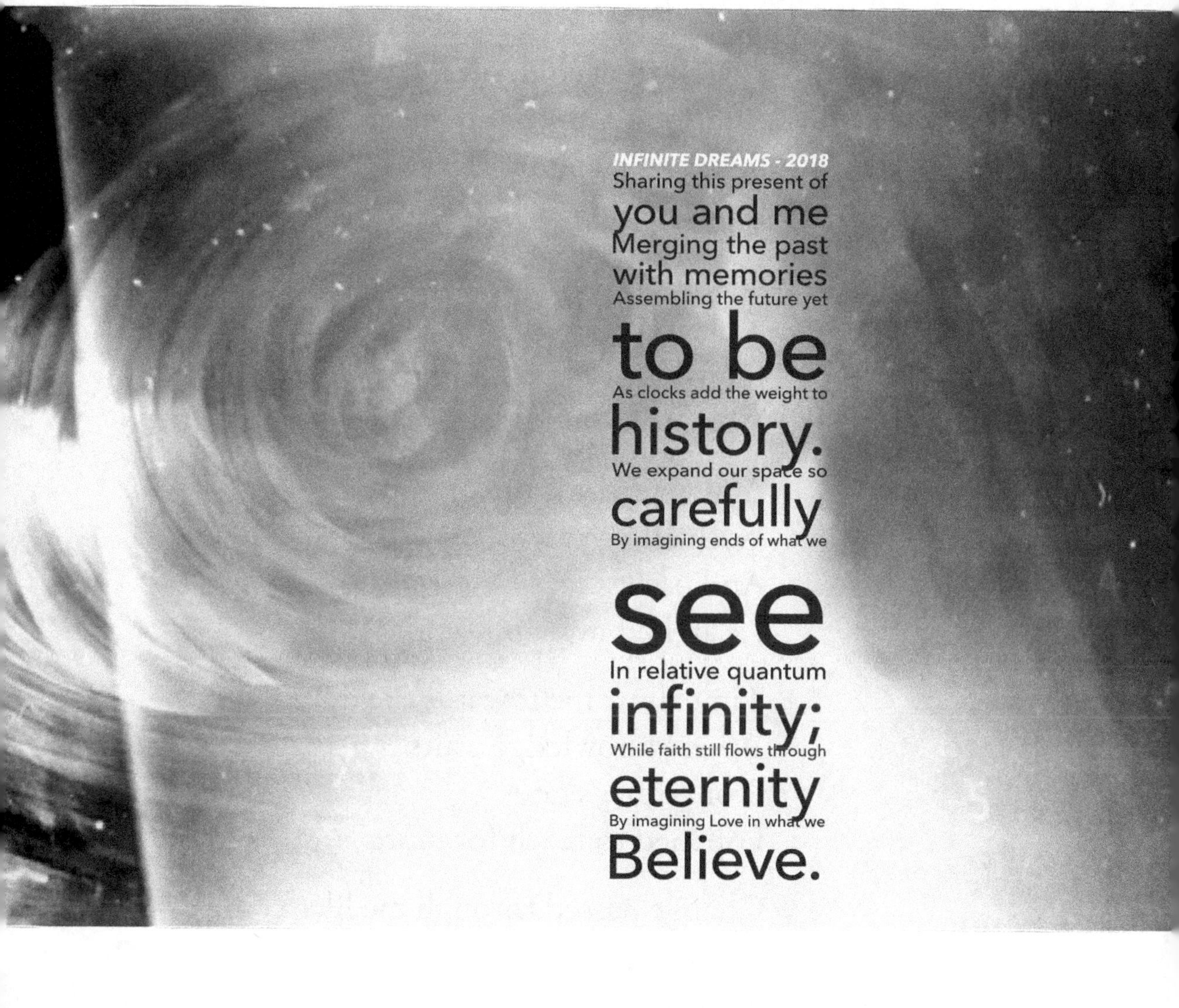

INFINITE DREAMS - 2018

Sharing this present of
you and me
Merging the past
with memories
Assembling the future yet
to be
As clocks add the weight to
history.
We expand our space so
carefully
By imagining ends of what we
see
In relative quantum
infinity;
While faith still flows through
eternity
By imagining Love in what we
Believe.

My Will

—1994 Sylvia Lynne

I awoke to a cold, sunny day
And found hope and delight
In seeing its light
Reflected in a new way

Outside tender branches of trees
Barren and slow
From the ice and the snow
Were waltzing in the breeze.

A new season wore on my face
With all its years
And useless fears
I searched my soul for grace.

Time drew me towards the door.
Where knowledge waits
From other's fate
I opened to reach for more

Change passed through me like a chill
Then my heart grew warm
To insight born
And I knew that growth was my will.

GRAVITY CITATIONS

Some of Lynne's artwork has been updated for this publication using Microsoft AI Copilot.
All photos are courtesy of Pixabay Contributors and Firefly Artists.

Firefly_Gemini Flash Rendered Image, pp. 146-47

Image by Nicolás from Pixabay, pp. 148-49

Image by Maria Karysheva from Pixabay, p. 150

Image by James Wheeler from Pixabay, pp. 152-53

Images by Wolfgang Eckert from Pixabay, pp. 154, 160

Image by Benjamin Balazs from Pixabay, p. 155

2012 Lynne's Oil Painting, p. 157

Image by candoyi from Pixabay, pp. 158-59

Image by Beverly Buckley from Pixabay, p. 159,

2012, 2018 Lynne's Original Oil Painting Integrated with Digital Painting, p. 158, 163

1994, 1988 -Lynne's Oil Paintings on Canvas, p. 158, 161, 162

Image by Anasouza00 from Pixabay, 164, 165

AWI - adventure writers ink & Station WIL

About the Authors

||| Three Sisters |||
CS Norwood, SL Malvoso, and
KI Sutphin

KI Sutphin, author of *Face to the Rain*, graduated from Elizabethtown College with a Bachelor of Science degree in Chemistry. After working as an educator, a chemist, and a computer programmer, she dedicated 25 years to IBM in various technical and marketing roles. On retiring from her assignment as a software engineering manager, she focused on her favorite hobbies, golf, photography, and writing fiction.

CS Norwood, author of the short stories and poems included in *The Storied Trail* holds a Master of Science degree from the University of South Alabama. She is a writer, editor, researcher, and indie publisher currently living in south Alabama. Her genres of choice are adventure and mystery stories, whether true-life or fiction. Her time is spent writing, researching, and helping others complete and publish their adventure books under AWI adventure writers ink or their individual imprint.

SL Malvoso is a Florida-based writer and visual artist whose work blends introspection with a sense of cosmic wonder in *Gravity*. Through poetry, digital painting, and reflective prose, she creates intimate, atmospheric pieces that invite readers to pause, breathe, and consider the unseen rhythms of time and space.

www.ingramcontent.com/pod-product-compliance
Lightning Source LLC
LaVergne TN
LVHW081318110826
845149LV00006B/1540

* 9 7 9 8 9 9 2 4 3 0 5 8 5 *